GOLD LEAF

Also by Robert Clarkson:

Headlong into the Sea – 1995

GOLD LEAF

A Story of
Britannia

Robert Clarkson

Buckland Publications Ltd
Barwick Road, Dover CT17 0LG

Monarchy is the gold filling in the mouth of decay.

John Osborne: *The Pendulum Years*, 1976

First Published 2000

ISBN 0 7212 0942 4

Printed in England by Buckland Press Ltd,
Barwick Road, Dover CT17 0LG

CONTENTS

ILLUSTRATIONS

PROLOGUE

WEDNESDAY, 7TH JANUARY 1959, was a good day to go. The water in the basin rippled under the cold north wind and a leaden sky hung over the dockyard. A television unit and a NAAFI van shared the jetty with a few families. On the upper deck of the royal yacht the band in greatcoats played the old tunes used when the big warships leave harbour.

At the entrance a second band on the Sally Port strained to be heard; a few children and their minders waved stoutly into the wind. 'Will Ye No Come Back Again' and the 'Post Horn Gallop' came thinly across the water. On the other side of the channel a seaman bugler at Fort Blockhouse sounded the alert in salute to the senior officer passing the Flag Officer Submarines. Portsmouth dropped astern.

Britannia was off round the world for the second time in three years. 'Bring us back a parrot,' the dockyard mateys used to shout when the old *Victoria and Albert III* left Portsmouth for her annual cruise to Cowes. In the coming eight months this yacht would steam 40,232 miles.

The day had begun agreeably for her admiral:

From:- Admiralty to Flag Officer Royal Yachts

Personal for Vice-Admiral P. Dawnay, CB, MVO, DSC.

You are promoted to Vice-Admiral to date 7th January 1959.

The day was not so good for the new boys.

Diary 7th January 1959:

Heavy swell from NW; few in wardroom for dinner and film cancelled. Motion is like a lift going up and down at a brisk pace. Even some old hands seasick.

I had served in her for four months; this was my first day at sea. It had taken me some time to get there, beginning on a memorable afternoon in Bow Street magistrates' court three years before. I set down the record of this long prelude to show how the process of selection for *Britannia* appointments sometimes worked. I was a pupil barrister waiting for my master's case to come on, one of the naval officers given legal training to enable their lordships to counter the criticism in the tabloid press that justice in the Royal Navy might be done but was not always seen to be done. A qualified barrister who had not practised was like a surgeon who had not operated but that is to miss the point. We were trained to meet a political rather than a legal reqirement. The critics would have to acknowledge that the navy had tried to do better.

Two of us sat behind Reggie's broad back and bald head. It had been a longish lunch. It was said at the Bar that Reggie Seaton accepted naval pupils because he had warmed to nautical matters as a young man in a Cambridge college boat – and believed that all naval officers drank gin. He was a charming and considerate master with deep knowledge of the practice of the criminal law. We thrived under his convivial tutelage, particularly at lunchtime, when reminded of life in the wardroom of a happy ship. There were occasions, as at sea, when there were anniverseries and the like to celebrate. This had been one of those days.

The stipendiary magistrate nodded towards Reggie and waited

for him to open the prosecution. He turned slowly on his bench and addressed me in a clear voice which travelled from one end of the court to the other.

'Are we in this?'

'Yes.'

When it was over our defeated team gathered in the corridor. Reggie was too big a man to give a damn about life's trivia and the conversation carried on around his clerk, just arrived from chambers.

'Conference confirmed with DPP's man at 5.30.'

'Good. That all?'

'Yes, Mr Seaton. One other thing.' He pulled out a scrap of paper. 'Would Mr Clarkson ring this number at the Admiralty before six?'

The message did not surprise me. I had spent the last three years around the Temple and was due for another job. The voice the other end began with a quick reminder that my interest in the law began with the Naval Discipline Act.

'We want you to drop what you are doing and come to the Admiralty as secretary to the Deputy Controller.'

'I have just done three years at this end of the Strand. Why two more years now at the other end?'

Silence. I could guess the unspoken answer – do as you are told and spare us the discussion.

'Who is the admiral?'

'Durnford-Slater.'

'Good.'

'He is leaving a month after you get here. Peter Dawnay is relieving him. He has asked for you.'

I realised then, long before it could happen, that I might go to *Britannia* should Rear-Admiral Dawnay become Flag Officer Royal Yachts. Flag officers could choose their secretaries; we had served together when he commanded the Third Destroyer

11

Squadron in the Mediterranean. The admiral in *Britannia* would not be eligible for relief until 1958 but Peter Dawnay was a likely contender. He had been on the staff which went to Canada with the King and Queen in 1939. Among the dwindling number of aristocrats on the Navy List, he was related by marriage to the royal family. Until recently he had commanded the six-inch cruiser *Glasgow*.

Accordingly, I went to the office of the Third Sea Lord, Controller of the Navy, responsible for ship building and repair. *Britannia* was never mentioned. I travelled the country with my boss, checking on the warships in the yards.

The Suez operation enlivened the routine. The admiral went to New York to support the Foreign Secretary at the United Nations and in his absence the task of organising the clearance of the wrecks in the canal fell on his desk, at the last moment, when the naval staff thought of it.

The Admiralty had plenty of senior officers with long experience of proper wars but none of them was ordered to take up this poisoned chalice. The Vice Chief of Naval Staff was in charge of this war but he was on summer leave and that may have been a factor. The captain who headed the Boom Defence and Salvage Department and I found ourselves alone with the First Lord and his private secretary. We were there to get a decision that only he could make. Lord Hailsham opened the ball.

'I understand you are a barrister. State your case.'

This was too good to miss. 'The Director will explain the technical issues, sir. On general grounds, I believe we have underestimated Arab nationalism and the operation will not be a success.'

This led to a vigorous monologue aimed at putting right this unknown from the cellars. It was heady stuff while it lasted.

After Suez the ship-builders made a killing with super-tankers because the Cape route called for such ships. Naval construction lost priority. I remember one Clydeside yard building a frigate. The admiral said he would like to see how *Jaguar* was getting on but his request was sidelined. When the car took us away I told the driver to make a detour. He took us to a pile of rusty plates shaped like a house of cards. There were no workmen there. When we got closer a party of rooks flew squawking from her bridge.

On the way back from one of these trips the admiral said that he was going to *Britannia* and asked whether I would like to go with him. I knew that the question might arise but had no ready answer. I said I would like time to consider; I had four sons to educate and knew that I should have to leave the navy soon. My next appointment would probably be my last. I had not served at sea for four years and was looking forward to a ship in the fleet.

This was not what the admiral expected. 'There is a tremendous cachet to a job in the yacht. I should hesitate to let it go.'

A visit to the oracle was indicated. I called on Reggie and told him that I planned to resign my commission and practise at the Bar.

'Where will you go if you stay on?'

'*Britannia.*'

'I suggest you consult your psychiatrist.'

That is how it happened.

H.M. Yacht BRITANNIA,
at Portsmouth.

30th December, 1959.

ROYAL YACHT MEMORANDUM NO.127

WEARING OF BLACK SATIN TIES

From 1st May, 1960, I should like all Officers in the Yacht to wear black satin ties with day uniform.

This was an old V.& A. custom.

[signature]

VICE-ADMIRAL

Distribution

All Officers.

Plate 1: A decree on officers' ties, December 1959

Chapter 1

ROUND THE WORLD CRUISE, 1959 –
PORTSMOUTH TO RANGOON

BRITANNIA HAD SIX COMMANDERS, heading the executive, engineering, navigation, electrical, medical and supply and secretariat departments. Her displacement made her a captain's command but she had an admiral for the job, a distinction not shared by any other ship so far as I am aware. This is not to say that admirals have never taken command if they felt like it. I remember a fraught occasion in the Tagus River when my admiral took over the flagship in a hurry because he decided that the captain lacked the ship-handling skill the situation needed.

Britannia's admiral was appointed 'Flag Officer Royal Yachts'. This was the custom and no reason was seen to change it although there would never again be more than one yacht. It was a reminder that *Britannia* was a unique ship in a service with a long history. A smart destroyer joined *Victoria and Albert III's* escort in the twenties and signalled 'Good morning,' in well-mannered submission. The reply was; 'This is not a good morning ship'. She was just different.

It is interesting to compare her with *Carlisle*, a light cruiser of comparable size in which I had served:

	Carlisle	*Britannia*
Displacement	5,390 tons (loaded)	4,715 tons
Command	Captain	Vice-Admiral
Length	450 ft	412 ft
Shaft Horsepower	40,000	12,000
Beam	43 ft	55 ft
Complement	400 (war)	240
Commanders	1 (Engineer Officer)	6
Wardroom	20 (war)	23
Designed speed	29 knots	21 knots

Britannia had no armament, even a saluting gun, to compare with *Carlisle's* 4x4" twin HA/LA multiple pom-pom, 6 Oerlikon, radars, directors, searchlights, fire-control systems, smoke floats, small arms, etc.

Britannia's design was based on that of a Harwich-Hook ferry. Her modest horse power was sustained by a commander, lieutenant-commander and three lieutenants of the engineering specialisation and sixty-five engine room ratings. Seventy trained seamen were there to work the upper deck, keep her clean and provide crews for her boats. Her poor relations steaming back and forth across the North Sea could never have shown a profit if manned to that scale. Much of the available accommodation in Britannia was used for royal vistors and their staffs so that space for the ship's company was modest. My cabin as a commander was no bigger than I had as a lieutenant in *Carlisle*. However, the plumbing was better, there was no anti-flooding sill across the door and the scuttle had not been welded up.

The entry for officers to the royal yacht was once rigorously selective; in Queen Victoria's time the names of three lieutenants from a waiting list of volunteers were submitted by the Admiralty to the Flag Officer Royal Yachts and sent on by him to the Queen, who picked one of them. The lobbying by those on the waiting list was intense. Some of the lucky ones remained in touch with the sovereign, notably in the time of George V, and attained high rank. Admiral Evan-Thomas, who commanded the 5th Battle Squadron at Jutland and became a central figure in the controversy following the battle, was one of them. Until 1923 'yacht' promotions were given to officers who had served there. In modern times the appointment of a head of department still required the sovereign's personal approval.

Arbitrary uniform rules were introduced; probably few have survived. In my time the admiral indicated that officers should wear black satin ties in day uniform, buy their caps from Herbert Johnson and stop wearing link buttons with mess undress jackets. We began drinking the Queen's health standing, unlike the rest of the navy who had drunk it sitting for generations; this change was sponsored by Lord Mountbatten.

Such nonconformities of custom and dress were not trivial; they emphasised her status as a ship apart from the fleet and an intention to keep her there by the senior officer who had the transitory power to introduce them. I am not convinced that they were beneficial. The Royal Navy had traditions of its own; the highest compliment it could pay to the sovereign was to run the yacht as far as possible like any other ship of the fleet. Cosmetic changes were divisive if they stressed a difference between yacht service and general service. Some would call them outlandish; imagine a regiment or battalion of the Household Brigade which would think it fitting to change its officers' uniforms or long held mess rules because they needed to remind the rest of the army that they were responsible for the life of the sovereign.

This narrative would be less than complete if I did not now report that in my time there was an unspoken interest in whether yacht officers were socially OK. These were the days of the late Dartmouth entry and the removal of the public school hurdle. The badges of acceptability having been thus brutally torn away it was a matter for conjecture whether everyone in the wardroom would be able to cut the social mustard. One young man obviously thought not and told a senior member of the household that the wardroom was nothing special; he was the only Etonian there. All this should not be taken too seriously. I believe however that when the admiral introduced his officers to Herbert Johnson and silk ties he was not directing their attention to their dress sense alone.

Diary 11th January, 1959 – Gibraltar

Arrived Gibraltar an hour too soon and, as we passed the breakwater, received signal 'do not enter harbour'. Too late. Our berth occupied by a tug which scuttled out as we came up. Confusion caused by mix-up in time zones in our arrival signal.

The long cruise ahead began auspiciously for me at Gibraltar where I was welcomed by John and Frances Stanton. They were old friends and it was good to see them. John was second-in-command of the battalion of the Royal Sussex which garrisoned the Rock. He had been severely wounded and captured at Alamein and now had a quiet number; me too. The difference between us was that he was still paid to fight if needed; I was out of the ring. This was an unavoidable downside to yacht service that must have been felt occasionally by some of those in it though I never heard it talked about. The cachet of being there at all was terrific but an unarmed yacht, however exalted, was not what had brought people into the navy.

Britannia was not in the *Victoria and Albert III's* class for elegance but when she entered harbour the world stopped to look at her dark blue hull, white upperworks, buff funnel and three raked masts. This combination was much used by warships in hot climates. Her paintwork absorbed the spectator, who might otherwise have sniffed at her short forecastle and shoe box topside aft.

The arrival at Gibraltar was spoiled. It was too much to have the same again at Malta. She came towards the entrance with the hands fallen in, the band at the ready and crowds at St Elmo waiting for the show. Her progress was abruptly barred by the merchantman *Argentina*, out of Syracuse for Valletta, who pushed in ahead and turned on her anchors in the middle of the fairway. *Britannia* had to go 120 revolutions astern to avoid a collision. The irritation caused by this episode was compounded by a silly signal from the C-in-C, whose staff could easily have avoided it had they been on the ball.

The Admiral Superintendent of Malta Dockyard was John Lee-Barber, a renowned destroyer officer who had commanded the 4th Destroyer Squadron in the Home Fleet when I was there. I showed him round in silence until we reached the quarter deck.

'That hatch cover,' said Johnny.

'What about it ?'

'Scruffy. Needs changing.'

At a lunch party at his house near the dockyard, a white cockatoo shared the proceedings, hopping on the admiral's shoulder from time to time and lungeing for the food.

Captain J. S. Dalglish, who had taken the yacht on her shake down cruise from Portsmouth to Malta in May 1954, was serving there and organised a yacht officers' reunion dinner at the Phoenicia Hotel. He had asked for 'wardroom wishes' to be signalled ahead under one of three categories:

'(a) very young unmarried,
(b) attractive deserted wives,
(c) of more mature age,
but of course surplus makes no handicap.'

Nigel, our engineer officer and wardroom social secretary, had to answer. He was used to dealing with a complaining bunch but this time he had no difficulty.

The party was alpha and the night before we left found us

dancing. My partner, a front runner in category (b) of the Dalglish formula, offered to drive me down to Grand Harbour. The fleet had long gone so the harbour was deserted. There were no boats or dghaisas anywhere. The waterfront cafes and bars were shut. Nothing moved. Lascaris steps were as quiet as a tomb. It was about 1am. I rang the officer of the watch.

'Please send a boat to Lascaris for me.'

'All boats are hoisted sir.'

'Well, lower one.'

'I am sorry but the commander has ordered that no more boats be lowered.'

I said good bye and thanked her for the lift.

'What are you going to do? You cannot walk up and down this jetty all night. You had better come back with me and I'll run you down in the morning.'

'You are very kind but that is not on. Peter is away.'

'So what? The neighbours will have nothing to talk about.'

'The neighbours don't know it.'

'For God's sake get in. I'm freezing.'

Next morning, early because we were sailing, I waited by the door for my good Samaritan to appear.

'Sorry to keep you hanging about but my car keys have disappeared. They must be somewhere in the hall here.'

They were not. Neither were they in her coat, bag, lost in a chair, in the kitchen, bathroom, behind a chair or on the floor. They were nowhere at all. They had simply vanished, taken away by the Devil himself for sport.

'Can I ring for a taxi?'

'Hopeless. They never come for hours.'

'I'll walk it.'

'Too far. No time.'

'Have one more look upstairs.'

If my naval career was ending it would do so with ridicule. I imagined what the headlines would be. The tabloids would not know where to start. Missed his ship on sailing? An officer? A commander? The royal yacht? And what about the *Times of Malta*? My innocent companion lived on this blasted island with her husband.

I heard footsteps racing down the stairs.

'Got them. In the loo.'

I sprinted across the jetty to the last boat and was back on board with thirty minutes to spare. It sounds a lot. I can only report that it seemed nothing then. On the bridge the atmosphere was genial at the thought of departure.

'Malta not what it was sir,' from the yeoman.

'I was lucky. I have a few friends here.'

We left in style and cleared Grand Harbour entrance at 14 knots. The staff at Malta were uncertain about our reception at Port Said. In the Suez operation, two years before, Britain, France and Israel had bombed and invaded Egypt upon a pretext. We were told that we could not rely on goodwill there now.

We were given royal treatment. Jim Cairo, the old Admiralty agent, boarded while we were under way, collected our mail and took orders for fresh food for delivery at Suez. We led the convoy. The El Firdan bridge was specially opened for us. In Lake Timsah the ship was allowed to anchor while the northbound convoy passed; the rest of our southbound convoy were sent to gare up (secure to the shore) in the Farouk Cut.

The canal was being widened and deepened everywhere. The fellaheen in long ant-like columns, each with a headbasket of earth, did the work. It was a buoyant, confident scene. The international brouhaha after Suez had changed nothing if our passage was anything to go by. In the Red Sea I began a closer look around.

The royal apartments were kept up to scratch when the household staff were not there by a handful of RN ratings under the Lieutenant Keeper and Steward of the Royal Cabins,

Lieutenant William Pardy. Bill was then in his sixties and had served in the old *V and A* for many years. He was a gentle, quiet man who had seen it all before and had become something of a legend. At Jutland he took the place of the Commander-in-Chief's Chief Steward, left behind on a shopping trip when *Iron Duke* sailed for the battle. He attended on Lord Jellicoe throughout the day and the following night, taking whatever he needed to the bridge and spotting top. In a quiet Hampshire burr he recalled the misty day in the North Sea when the last fleet action between ships of the line was fought and six thousand from our side did not come back.

His naval career began in 1910 when he was in Portsmouth looking for work. He heard that the captain of a Dreadnought battleship had a vacancy for a steward. He put on his bowler hat and suit, boarded one of her boats, asked for an interview with the captain and got the job. He did not wear uniform on duty, being a non-continuous service rating and not entitled to it. He described the relationship between the captain and his assistant steward as that of squire and footman. The captain had a large heavy book, like a family bible, which was secured with a lock. He was always reading it. One day he forgot to lock it and Bill peeped inside. Each page held a plump naked lady with the head cut out and the head of a female member of the royal family put in its place.

Diary 26th January 1959 – Aden.

Went to Crater – the native quarter where things were supposed to be cheaper. Narrow, filthy streets teeming with all races. No local products. Only trade is in the retail of British goods. We arrived the day the new assembly started session. Much disaffection. Recent port strike just over. We are on the way out here. Too many coming in and no work for them. The mob is pro-Nasser or communist.

Plate 2: 27th January 1959 – AB Clench with the 28lb grouper

The cricket team began with an hour's trip across Aden Bay inan open boat with a Somali crew because the RAF transport did not turn up.

Diary 27th January 1959 – Aden

We fielded first and Rodney made me bowl. Concrete and matting wicket. No. 1 left with split finger, No. 3 yorked and 4 bowled with a slower one. They declared at 132 for 5. We got them.
Oil company general manager delighted with a ship's crest we gave them for their clubhouse. RAF transport did not turn up again and they sent us back in their bus. Yachtsmen thanked their hosts individually. Hosts impressed.
Back in time to see AB Clench, the CPO's messman, land a 28 lb grouper from the gangway. All came to watch. Fish borne in triumphant procession to the f'c'stle.

Our programme meant four months of almost continuous steaming and a boiler clean somewhere in the Indian Ocean. At the planning stage Colombo and Karachi were proposed and turned down by Sri Lanka and Pakistan on political grounds. We learned en route that it was to be Vizagapatam in south-east India, some 3000 miles from Aden.

Britannia's ship's company was accustomed to substantial periods at sea without the ardours of a warship routine. They were not called upon for turret drills and seamanship evolutions. The relationship between all rates was relaxed without over-familiarity. Everyone knew his job and wanted to keep it. They wore black bows on the backs of their bell bottoms because that had been the rig in Queen Victoria's yachts. They accepted such oddities for the privilege of joining an elite.

Between Aden and Vizagapatam, with no royal standard at her mainmast, the upper deck was occupied by deck hockey players

24

and physical training classes. The admiral dined the wardroom in two batches and the band played whenever they were asked. It was near to the routine of a cruise liner for those with no watches to keep, without the luxury. Peter, our popular and relaxed doctor, overplayed his hand and turned in in one of the staff cabins in the empty royal end of the yacht. He was running a temperature and thought that the air-conditioning there would help him to sleep. A steward put a 'Do Not Disturb' notice on the door. Unfortunately for him the admiral made one of his rare tours aft and ignored the notice, anxious to know who had broken the rule that his personal permission was needed; *lèse-majesté* was a cardinal offence in the service upon which we were engaged.

'What does *lèse-majesté* mean?'

'In your case, Peter, presumptuous conduct on the part of an inferior. This is not a destroyer.'

Vizagapatam had a scenic, narrow entrance surrounded by wooded hills. To the north the bay was an arc of shimmering sand backed by Hindu temples, white houses and palm trees. Fishing dugouts with triangular sails were hauled up the beach before the rough huts of their owners.

The yacht was the guest of *Circars*, the Boys' Training Establishment for the Indian Navy. Their hospitality was embarrassing. The results of the team games were about even, save for the officers' tennis. They had two charming lieutenants who buried the wardroom, two by two, and then asked, with no hint that the result was foregone, whether anyone else would care for a set.

The officers were kept hard at it with balls, dinners and receptions organised by our naval hosts and the American and British staffs of the oil companies. The committee at the Waltair Club, where the jungle was getting very close and the polo cups, billiard tables and old photographs were covered with dust, had refused an offer by an oil company to have a swimming pool built for them. The regiments had gone but for the surviving British members it seemed as if the change was temporary. We were asked to sing songs round the piano and play slosh with them on the faded tables.

Four of us were invited to shoot wildfowl at first light on an up-country lake. The brass pots on the heads of the women shimmered in the dawn light amidst the fires of the rickshaw drivers starting their day. Sleeping bodies lay everywhere. On the lake we crouched singly in small canoes while an enthusiastic Indian in the stern paddled towards the duck. He needed skill to get over the water lilies to retrieve the game; we needed luck not to capsize her or shoot the boatman when wrestling to reload. On the water's edge two black oily pillars of smoke marked funerals.

Admiral of the Fleet Lord Fraser, who was coming with us as a guest of Prince Philip, joined by train, arriving shortly before midnight. He ran the wardroom to earth at a reception ashore and became the life and soul of the party. After a week of night life the rest of us were ready to leave at the appointed time but his enthusiasm and general *joi de vivre* refreshed everyone, hosts included, until dawn.

Before we left for Rangoon our admiral presented the commodore of the Indian navy with 'The Britannia Cup' for a competition of their choice and as a memento of our visit. If it had been a qualified success it was not the fault of the Indians, who had been splendid hosts. The nine days at Vizagapatam were intended to provide a break as well as a boiler clean but the facilities ashore for the yachtsmen, in a city of 100,000 people in grinding poverty, with beer at five shillings a bottle, were not good.

Diary 14th February, 1959 – at sea, Vizagapatam to Rangoon.

Admiral talked to ship's company after church and explained and apologised about Vizag. Their reaction was dour.

Lord Fraser was a welcome visitor to the wardroom. He had a remarkable memory for names and people. He told me that he had run into my cousin at Colombo and had a long talk with him about his days in command of an MTB. I had a cousin at that time in the Queen's Flight and for a moment I thought he was confused. I remembered in the nick of time that he must have met my wife's brother, then a tea broker in Sri Lanka. Every word the admiral said about him (except his relationship to me), gleaned in the course of a few minutes conversation in a room full of people, was accurate.

Diary 17th February, 1959 – Rangoon.

Embarked naval attaché and two Irrawaddy pilots at 0800 and started up the river for Rangoon. Tide runs very fast and locals reckon that if you fall in you do not come out. Secured to a buoy off Lewis Street Jetty at 1130. Landed at 1240 with Rodney, Neil and cricket team. In a rickety bus to university where we played in boiling heat against Mr Ishmail's XI. He was an ageing Indian in a topee who runs a travel agency. Back on board at 1800. White waistcoat and stiff shirt and then to reception given by Commodore Than Pe, their chief of naval staff. Usual whisky and small eats, held in a garden of Ministry of Defence. Soldiers all over the place. Prime Minister has just resigned, there is no successor and political situation tense.

Lord Fraser called on the Prime Minister and landed in uniform with a flag lieutenant borrowed from the wardroom. It was a ceremonial occasion and the admiral was resplendent in his many orders and decorations. I asked flags how it had gone.

'The car was twenty minutes late.'

'What then?'

'He walked up and down the jetty surrounded by the mob as if nothing had happened. For something to say I pointed out that the exit from the jetty was called Fraser Road.

' "Yes," he said, "my father was a sapper. He laid this place out." '

Rangoon stirred imperial memories. The savage midday heat and the fiery tempers of the men, allegedly ready with a knife to answer an insult, lived with their gentle Buddhism, dreamlike pagodas and enchanting women. Here reality matched the poetry:

By the old Moulmein Pagoda, lookin' eastward to the sea,
There's a Burma girl a-settin', and I know she thinks o' me;
For the wind is in the palm-trees, an' the temple-bells they say:
'Come you back, you British soldier; come you back to Mandalay!'
 Come you back to Mandalay,
 Where the old flotilla lay:
 Can't you 'ear their paddles chunkin' from Rangoon to Mandalay?
 On the road to Mandalay,
 Where the flyin'-fishes play,
 An' the dawn comes up like thunder outer China 'crost the Bay!

I gave a day's leave to a chief petty officer who had been asked by his mother to take a photograph of his brother's grave. He had been buried near Rangoon in the fighting in 1944. He found the place. I asked him how his brother had been killed.

'Local hooch,' he said, 'They were warned about it and took no notice.'

Diary 18th February, 1959 – Rangoon

Ashore at 0800 wth Nigel, Philip and Geoff for tour of Shwe Dagon (the Golden Pagoda) with our Burmese liaison officer, a Dartmouth trained young chap who kept up a line of cheerful repartee. 2000 year old pagoda towers to heaven, covered in gold leaf. Men kneel to pray and women sit. They

28

pray at various positions round the pagoda, depending on the day of the week on which they were born. One of the main offerings is water, a sign of purity. The precincts of the pagoda are washed daily by volunteers. Good thing because no one is allowed to wear anything on their feet when looking round.

Yacht moved at 1200 three miles downstream to comply with the port regulation that no ship may sail at night above the dangerous Monkey Point Shoal. Our motor cutter, filled with Prince Philip's baggage, followed us down and took a short cut over the Shoal in five feet of water and just cleared it. HRH joined at 2300 after a month's tour of India and Pakistan and we left at once for Singapore. Sir Alexander Grantham, expert on W. Pacific and ten years governor of Hong Kong, Lord Fraser, Dr Breitling (friend of HRH) and staff of Orr, (secretary) and Severne (equerry) also there. Admiral Gladstone (C-in-C Eastern Fleet) coming as far as Singapore.

Chapter 2

ROUND THE WORLD CRUISE, 1959 –
RANGOON to HONG KONG

BY A STRANGE IRONY, *BRITANNIA,* a symbol of British prestige, called on this cruise at the great coaling stations of the *Pax Britannica.* Gibraltar, Malta, Aden, Singapore, Hong Kong and Bermuda were once bases that reinforced the sea power that had won and kept the British Empire. When *Britannia* arrived with flags and ceremony, the warships there were in symbolic numbers only; she was an actress walking on the stage to a deserted auditorium.

Many, perhaps most, on board her in 1959, had lived through the national decline and remembered the prime ministerial assurance that he had no intention of presiding over the demise of the British Empire. The reality was that two world wars had taken the money and many of the men who ran it. The empire had long been a dirty word among intellectuals at home, capitalists in the New World and marxists in the Old. The Atlantic Charter was an early reminder that Hitler was more sympathetic towards it than Roosevelt. Without a peace in 1940 it had no future.

Some would say that the end was inevitable and the Suez fiasco, nearly three years before, was just another milestone on a downhill road that history ordained from the beginning.

Far-called our navies melt away –
On dune and headland sinks the fire–
Lo, all our pomp of yesterday
Is one with Nineveh and Tyre !

Grand Admiral Doenitz, in his final message to his heroic submariners, had the last word: 'Churchill, the gravedigger for English power'.

At Singapore we were met by the Eastern Fleet, successors to *Prince of Wales* and *Repulse*, sunk at Kuantan in 1941, *Exeter* and her squadron, overwhelmed in two actions in the Java Sea in 1942, and the fleet based on Trincomalee in 1943-45.

The ships came towards us in two columns, the cruiser *Ceylon* (Captain F. R. Twiss, DSC) with the Australian frigates *Queenborough* and *Quiberon* forming the port column, and the destroyers *Cheviot* and *Cavalier,* with the frigate *Chichester,* the starboard column. They were under the tactical command of Frank Twiss, a survivor from *Exeter*. After a 21-gun royal salute from each ship both columns steamed down either side of the yacht on opposite courses and wheeled into single line ahead on our starboard quarter. *Ceylon* then led them closely down our starboard side, manned at their guardrails by their ships' companies, cheering in turn as they passed HRH, who took the salute from the royal deck. It could not have been better done.

As I write the navy is reduced to little more than forty thousand men, women and marines to rule the waves. The squadron led by *Ceylon* that day stays in the memory; if the ships had to go they would do it in style:

Proud, open-eyed,
Laughing to the tomb.

Britannia anchored in Man o' War Roads, Singapore, and dressed overall, the flags running from her stern, over the tops of

31

her three masts, down to her bows. The faster they went up the better it looked. The Supply Division led by Chief Writer Barrett manned the lines. A local newspaper reported that the hoist had been made 'in seconds by machinery'.

Singapore was clean and prosperous, without the dejection of January 1942 or the Japanese detritus of January 1946, when I was there before. *Britannia*, as always, aroused great interest and people one hardly knew rang up and openly sought a look-round.

The wardroom was entertained in style by a rich Chinese film maker, Mr Run Run Shaw. We enjoyed delicious Chinese food and danced in an air-conditioned cinema with the seats removed. Chinese starlets, in heavily brocaded cheong-sams, tittered when they tried their few English words on us. The competition for their attention was won easily by an American civilian who addressed them in fluent Mandarin.

When the ship left for Sarawak the jetty was solid with people, with a band and ceremonial guard-of-honour drawn from the three services. The water between us and the shore widened, the guard presented arms and the crowd cheered. On the yacht's upper deck the ranks of smart yachtsmen were motionless as she glided away. The ship, as always, made the big occasion. Measured against an aeroplane or train with red carpets, it was no contest.

Diary 26th February, 1959 – Kuching

Pilot embarked off Tanjong Po and took us up the Kuching River to an anchor off Tanjong Sadap. The jungle comes down to the wide river on both sides. The bank dotted with Sea Dyak huts on stilts over the water. The river is the main highway throughout the country.

Sarawak is the kind of place a young man might have in mind when thinking of joining the navy and seeing the world.

The yacht was met by a flotilla of decorated boats in a towed procession, including a dragon that needed three craft to support it. Launches with school children provided a foam of waving white hankerchieves in silent welcome. They did not make a sound. Noise on such occasions showed bad manners.

The doctor and I drew the long straws that evening and represented the wardroom at a private dinner given by the governor for Prince Philip. We set off up river into the setting sun on comfortable wicker chairs fitted in the bows of the boat. It was a four mile journey to Pending where cars took us on through lines of waving Chinese. At Kuching we boarded a white gondola driven by four kneeling paddlers for the short stretch to Astana, at one time the family home of the Brookes, the White Rajahs of Sarawak, and now the residency of the governor. The river was bright with lights from the upperworks of a ferry – the *Rajah Brooke* – alongside nearby. From the water gate through the garden to the house the path was lit by flaring torches. The governor, Sir Roland Turnbull, KCMG, gave a garden reception for 500 people after the dinner.

The reception was followed by an exhibition of local dancing and a grand finale firework display where we were the guests of the Bishop of Sarawak. His garden was full of people he did not know; he thought they had come for the fireworks. He never locked his house.

Sometime after midnight Lord Fraser announced that he would visit the Chinese open market; Breitling, the doctor, and I went with him. The market was crowded with families, shopping or eating under glaring gas lights and a tropical moon. Lord Fraser and Breitling ordered chicken chop suey. The market included the odd abattoir or its local equivalent to ensure that the chickens were fresh.

The next leg took us 824 miles to Sandakan, North Borneo, where the Japanese had given the locals a bad time in the late war. Their ships were still told to anchor off when they came to load the hard wood. This was less disagreeable than it sounds; the current made the approach alongside difficult.

The yacht came towards a berth next to a flotilla of decorated boats, ready for the next day's regatta. Crowds of silent locals watched us from wooden stands, bobbing gently on pontoons, while the admiral and two commanders in the wing of the bridge orchestrated the entertainment involved in getting her alongside.

The British colony was reinforced by up-country members, some of whom had travelled for days through the jungle to see us. Prince Philip arrived back from his tour and the regatta began with water-sports, motorboat races and a decorated boat competition. The crowd roared its approval and waved flags. The Chinese are gamblers and the boat races excited them. One of the wooden stands began to bend wearily away from the pontoon. It disappeared slowly under the water to the shouts of the victims and the cheers of the rest.

The evening reception was followed by a din-dang, a Malayan marathon dance. It had three basic steps and continuous arm-swinging before a distant, changing partner. The music involved non-stop thumps from a drum and tinkles from a cow-bell. The wardroom did their best but did not stay the course. The din-dang continued for eight hours. An Anglo-Burmese chief inspector of police at the bar told me that it was his job to chase Philippino pirates in a motor launch with a Vickers gun. He and the din-dang were typical products of this exotic corner of Asia.

The course for the 1100 miles to Hong Kong took us across the Sulu Sea, less used then by shipping, and through the Linapakan Strait into the China Sea. In the morning watch after clearing the strait the yacht sounded four short blasts on her siren, alerting those still in their bunks. Noise was something we tried to avoid but this time there was no choice. In bright sunshine a Norwegian tanker had fixed on our port bow on a collision course. It was her duty by the Rules of the Road to alter out of our way but she showed no sign that she intended to do anything. We had to turn in a hurry. The general view was that her officer of the watch had switched to automatic and either gone to sleep or left the bridge to do some painting.

An escort of three frigates arrived out of thick fog, expected in Hong Kong waters at that time of year. It lifted as we entered harbour for the fifty hours the programme allowed. There was little time to waste.

Diary 6th March 1959 – Hong Kong.

Garden Party with North and Nigel. Government House is a hideous building built by Japanese – polished concrete blocks, inside like a public lavatory. 4,000 people there. We were in uniform. Admiral in morning coat. Rhona Churchill (journalist) nobbled me and asked the usual questions. She claims that yachtsmen have been spilling the beans to her ashore about Britannia.

As press officer I had no orders beyond a general remit to say no more than I had to. The press were not given handouts or verbal briefings. I was a bank guard dealing with potential bank robbers. It followed that journalists got their information where they could and felt under no obligation to check it too carefully.

Three of us went with Lord Fraser to Repulse Bay to lunch with a Chinese nationalist general he knew. The house had been built in 1931 to look like a Scottish Victorian shooting lodge. Antlers, armour, oak tables and vast fireplaces proliferated in a place a world away from a red deer. The owner was told by a soothsayer that he would die as soon as he stopped building. Thus the outside was littered with summerhouses, swimming pools and follies of all kinds. The co-operation between the soothsayer and the builder was probably close.

We were given chop sticks, face towels, birds nest soup and innumerable courses, ending with mango and a Havana cigar. There were a number of Chinese ladies there to whom we were not introduced.

The night before leaving two of us were entertained by Lieutenant-General Sir Eric Bastyan, the Commander British Land Forces. We were the last to leave and the general insisted that we take his car to see the night life in the colony. One night spot followed another, in descending order of sophistication. At the last one we were delighted to find the captain of one of the frigates with his first lieutenant and two Chinese girls. We collected drinks and went over to join them but they had gone. There were occasions when there was a certain wariness towards us but service in the royal yacht had no effect on our camaraderie with the real navy. We all knew that luck had brought most of us to where we were and we would soon be back in our boxes.

We left with the same frigate escort and a fly-past by Venoms of the Royal Air Force. The commander-in-chief's yacht *Alert* fired a royal salute off Tattony Point and *Britannia* pointed alone into the Pacific where she would be for the next forty days.

Plate 3:21 February 1959; Singapore escort

Plate 4: 1 March 1959; Sandakan – going alongside

Chapter 3

ROUND THE WORLD CRUISE – 1959
HONG KONG TO PORTSMOUTH

HONG KONG TO THE WESTERN SOLOMONS is 3,356 miles. We met monsoon weather north of Luzon on a night passage; the Philippines government had been refused a visit from the yacht and our man in Manilla, anxious not to have that denial recalled, asked *Britannia* to keep out of sight of land when passing his host country.

On the third day from Hong Kong typhoon *Sally* was reported 400 miles away on a converging course. We altered but she changed direction during the middle watch and by 0900 was 200 miles ahead and still coming our way. The wind and swell increased and we were drenched in fine rain, a classic portent of a serious blow. We slid past her and made a landfall on Yap Island.

Diary 15th March, 1959 – Hong Kong to Tench Island

RFA Wave Master *transferred 300 tons of oil and three tons of fresh provisions in a four hour replenishment at sea. I gave them the mail because they are going to Manus. She had left Christmas Island three weeks before to meet us. Church in the Royal Dining Room. Amazing sunset. Sea turned purple. Julie joined the scrum in the swimming bath.*

(The swimming bath was a canvas container filled with sea water rigged on the royal deck. It would hold three or four people, provided the horse-play was restrained. Julie and Anne were lady clerks from Buckingham Palace who had joined at Rangoon, and the only women on board. Anne had been round the world with Britannia on her 1956-57 cruise.)

The yacht was now in the Bismarck Archipelago, once a remote corner of the German Empire. Admiral von Spee's Pacific Squadron avoided it in August 1914. When the British looked for him here he was 1000 miles to the south, at Ponape in the Carolines. The primitive wireless of those days made intelligence of his whereabouts hard to get. He evaded his enemies in these wastes for four months, won a battle at Coronel, and was destroyed by a squadron led by two battle cruisers at the Falkland Islands. Retribution was inevitable from the beginning; his story has an honoured place in the history of the Imperial German Navy. It also had an important part in deciding German naval strategy in World War II. Admiral Raeder's admiration for von Spee's cruise led to the building of *Scharnhorst, Gneisenau, Bismarck* and *Tirpitz,* and the German cruiser warfare operations in 1939-41. Consequently the enemy could not mount a decisive U-boat offensive in those years. The heavy ship programme had been chosen instead. It is at least arguable that von Spee and his legendary squadron ensured that Britain survived in 1940-41.

Prince Philip decided to land on one of the islands. Tench is one mile long, three-quarters of a mile wide and uninhabited, according to the Admiralty pilot. Well-wooded and flat, from a mile away the trees seemed to grow out of the sea. Three of us crossed the shallows of the inner reef in a dinghy. A path took us from the beach through the jungle to the weather side of the island where the surf tumbled in. I avoided a disgusting creature the size of a fat mole without legs. Nigel said it was a sea slug. We followed another track and found a village and fifty three people (of whom all but three had never left it), and a head man in a loin cloth decorated with a Red Cross. He dealt with medical affairs between visits from a doctor, who called every eighteen months.

Their huts were built on stilts to avoid the land crabs who scuttled abundantly over the volcanic soil. They spoke English of a kind and were anxious to assure us that they had put on clothes when they saw our boats coming in. Perhaps a missionary had passed this way and rebuked them for their innocent nakedness. They showed no surprise and little interest in our sudden arrival and exuded tranquillity. There were signs of idiocy on some faces. Even if they had had bicycles, one answer to inter-breeding in remote communities in Victorian England, they had nowhere to pedal to.

They made outrigger canoes from the trees and lived on fish. Our civilisation was put into perspective when the head man said that we had nothing that they wanted except fish hooks.

We crossed the equator that day and during the night Dolphinius, clerk of the Court of King Neptune, arrived on the bridge to announce that the Crossing the Line ceremony would be held later, when the usual rites would take place. 'Usual' is misleading; the proceedings have no rules except one – all those run to earth are ducked by the bears in a canvas bath. The bears are drawn from the heftiest members of the ship's company and no one escapes the ducking, apart from the captain, those on watch and those with a certificate from King Neptune proving that they had crossed the line before. The last category offered no exemption in practice, the bears simply ignoring the certificates. The disciplined routine customary in Her Majesty's ships is reduced for several hours to an abandoned water rout with drowning the only bar. *Britannia* did not break any new ground.

Diary 17th March, 1959 – Tench Island to Gizo, Solomon Islands

1200 Buka Island on starboard beam. Crossing the line

ceremony all forenoon. Wardroom provided guard of honour for King Neptune and Queen Amphitrite. Rugger jerseys, swimming trunks, decorated bowler hats and broomhandle spears. Blackened faces. We marched on to the fo' castle armed with firecrackers outside and brandy and ginger inside, smoking cheroots. Prince Philip sat on the platform accompanied by Neptune and Amphitrite, the band played and their majesties inspected the guard. We lit the firecrackers with the burning cheroots. They exploded all over the place. Peter Robinson and I deafened, my fingers numbed. Don's shirt on fire and the air full of red paper. Everyone said it was most effective. The usual chaos followed. Special warrants for Lord Fraser (being the most senior bachelor in the navy etc), Prince Philip and the admiral, excused them from the treatment.

The rest then chucked in, including the two girls, Jim Orr and the guard. Rodney, caught as he went off watch, went in in uniform, shoulder straps and all. Only about 80 genuine novices who had not crossed the line before. Nigel skulked all forenoon on the bridge and came down at lunch time when he thought the coast was clear. We ducked him in fresh water in the wardroom bathroom, in uniform. He was indignant.

In April 1942, the navigating officer said that Emerald *had crossed the line three times during one forenoon when the Japs were chasing us round the Indian Ocean. Tell that to a bear. They do not give a damn.*

The British Solomon Islands Protectorate, where Sir Arthur Grimble was sent as a married Colonial Office cadet in 1913, no longer has the magic he described in *A Pattern of Islands*. Wars and the predatory economic policies of the west have seen to that. Wrecked Japanese ships and craft littered the beaches and the lagoons were scarred with old jetties built by the Americans. Our four day visit began at Gizo, in the Western Solomons.

41

Diary 18th March, 1959. At Gizo.

We went through a hideous collection of reefs to our berth with the help of the leading marks and buoys put down for us the month before by the survey ship HMS Cook. *Six war canoes came out, their crews dressed in white. On shore a red, white and blue decorated landing stage was filled with patient school children. Fifty black Melanesians in scarlet sarongs stood immobile. Shoals of glittering silver and white fish leaped out of the water in front of them. To seaward the two horns of the reef were smothered by the surf, bright in the sun. Thirty miles away, the top of a mountain marked another island.*

Gizo lives by the collection and export of dried copra. There were many inter-island boats about. The talk was of a recent disaster when a 300 tonner disappeared with all hands on a short trip to Malaita.

Death at sea is familiar in these islands. A new passenger boat had not been seen again. The Chinese owner had added an extra section to her hull when she was being built in Hong Kong and made her unstable.

The High Commissioner for the Western Pacific, Sir John Gutch, and Lady Gutch, embarked as guests of Prince Philip for the passage to Honiara and Christmas Island. Honiara was home to Henderson Field, a key position in the Solomons land battle in 1942, but we could not visit it because the river had washed a bridge away. The dark outline of Savo Island appeared across the channel. In a brilliant night action here on 9th August 1942 the Japanese navy sank the heavy cruisers HMAS *Canberra*, USS *Vincennes* and USS *Quincey* and answered the lie that they could not fight at night.

Prince Philip received deputations from nearby islands on the football field. The heat was numbing. The locals broke off palm leaves to bar the sun. When it was over we asked for a swim and were taken to a mill pond fed by a river. We thrashed about in the space available, between the devil and the deep blue sea, the river being occupied by crocodiles inland and the limitless Pacific by sharks, who had recently come closer and taken four swimmers, including an Australian visitor.

I met an elderly clergyman at Government House who had been in the Solomons since 1902. In those days a native feast was not complete without human flesh; heads were collected like stamps. We dined to the music of slippers beaten on hollow bamboo pipes and the thumping of bamboo staves on the hard earth. The local craze was *Tra La La* a new dance which allowed the partners to bump their sides together, raising concern among the missionaries, sensitive to the challenge of the flesh to their work in this Eden.

Malaita Island, our next stop, 93 miles on, is considered to have the most savage of all the native Solomon islanders. Many came down from the hills for our visit, armed with ironwood spears and bows with poisoned arrows. I suggested to the chief secretary that the weapon display had been laid on for the visitors.

'Not really. They killed two British officials and their escort with spears like that.'

'In Captain Cook's time?'

'1935.'

On the way in to Bina, our anchorage at Malaita, we found the inter-island steamer *Coral Queen* stuck on Alite Reef. *Britannia's* navigating officer, first lieutenant and boatswain took a party over and helped her to lay out a kedge anchor and haul herself off. Communication between the yacht and *Coral Queen* was by the inter-island broadcast, heard by every local with a radio. The listeners kept abreast of events about wires, tides and depths as the drama was played out. They had a bonus when the technical flow was interrupted abruptly by the voice of the commander in *Britannia*.

'*Coral Queen* from *Britannia*.'

'*Britannia* from *Coral Queen* – receiving you loud and clear.'

'This is the commander. Tell *Britannia's* navigating officer that he is the father of a daughter and we are waiting to wet the baby's head.'

It was a short wait. Our divers inspected her bottom and confirmed that she was unaffected save for a modest dent.

Graciosa Bay, an island in the Santa Cruz group, was our last call in the Solomons. The harbour provided one small patch shallow enough for the anchor to reach the bottom. The fathomless depths about us were in harmony with this strange place, the most unsophisticated of the islands we met, after Tench. The anchorage was encircled by a chain of villages decorated with leaves and flowers along the freshly brushed paths. The women were topless; the local culture was alive and kicking. The coxswain of the first boat ashore had the usual question to answer when he came back,

'Is it negative jumpers 'ere then, 'swain?'

'Not 'arf!'

The locals were friendly although it was obvious that western visitors were infrequent. Hillmen with the usual spears and poisoned arrows came to see the show and watch the dancing. A wild mountain man with shaggy hair, covered with tattoos, smoked an old pipe with a two inch silver band. Silver was unknown here. The island was discovered by the Spanish in 1590 and not found again for 200 years. I decided that his ancestor acquired the silver from the Spanish.

On the 22nd March we left Graciosa Bay for Tarawa, the first call in the Gilbert and Ellice Islands, oiling en route for the last time from *Wave Master*. Having her close alongside for the replenishment made a diversion from the tedium of the overcast days and constant swell. The Pacific Ocean is dull company.

Every department on board fielded a deck hockey team. The battles with rope grommets and walking sticks amid the hatches and ventilators of the upper deck dispelled the tedium. When the game reached the right level of competitive frenzy the shins of the opposition were hit as often as the grommet. Touch rugby on a carrier's flight deck, when the touching is abandoned in the heat of combat for tackling, is in the same category. Deck quoits and deck tennis were organised for the distinguished guests. Sometimes, when there was a vacancy, a lucky one or two managed to share the canvas bath with the delicious Julie and splashed about with her in innocent jolly good fun.

The day before Tarawa, HMNZS *Rotoiti*, a smart New Zealand frigate, joined the escort. Prince Philip was transferred by jackstay and hoisted his flag in her, the first time that an Admiral of the Fleet of the New Zealand navy had flown his flag in a New Zealand ship.

Tarawa is a series of low-lying inter-connected atolls, an important centre in the Gilbert and Ellice group and not new to Bill Pardy who announced that he had been here in 1919 with Lord Jellicoe on his round the world cruise in HMS *Iron Duke*. Bill added (the temptation must have been irresistible) that so far as he could make out nothing much had changed.

The local cricket team played in bare feet. I tried to york their opening bat and the ball landed with a loud smack, full toss on his foot. He did not move a muscle and played the next one as if nothing had happened. The Australian umpire told me that if he had shown any indication of discomfort, let alone pain, he would have become a figure of fun. We were well beaten but cheered up when we learned that one of their side had captained his college team at Christchurch University and played rugby against the British Lions.

The island may have a place in American history similiar to the one that Gallipoli has in ours. Tarawa was on a much smaller scale but suffered equally from inept planning. The 1944 assault was made with incorrect navigational data and the marines were sent in on an ebb tide. A three day prelimiminary bombardment failed to kill a single Japanese soldier in the deep defence works and the assaulting infantry had to wade ashore through broken coral pools and intense machine gun, mortar and artillery fire. The Japanese bunkers we were shown were ten feet thick.

On 27th March, 1959, Good Friday, we left for the short voyage to Ocean Island, a small volcanic outcrop whose phosphate deposits accounted for 48% of the income of the Gilbert and Ellice Islands. The history of its acquisition is unlike that for Canada, India or the Sudan. There was no Plains of Abraham, Plessey or Omdurman.

The Oxford Survey of the British Empire, 1914, Volume 5, page 482 explains:

The discovery of phosphates led to the inclusion of a number of islets in the British Empire which would not otherwise have been worth claiming. Ocean, Starbuck, Wreck Reef, Cato, Suwarrow, Bird, Jarvis, Enderbury and McKean's Islands have all been leased by the British Government to the Pacific Islands Company for terms sufficient to allow their phosphate deposits to be removed. When they are completely denuded they will, doubtless, sink back into their old remote isolation.

The approach to the island led past the wreck of the merchantman *Kelvinbank*, hanging on the reef after an error of judgement in 1951. There was no indigenous population; those there were phosphate workers and their families on short contracts. Around the harbour, hoppers, crushers and sheds littered the foreshore, while the roads were lined with spare bits of machinery, corrugated iron roofed sheds and debris. On the other side of the island the gardens of the old residency destroyed by the Japanese are now part of a golf course. There the hibiscus, frangipani and bougainvillaea stretch down the green hillside to the blue Pacific. The scent is heavy everywhere as it must have been when the Japanese collected every man, woman and child on the island in the garden, and shot them all so that they did not have to feed them.

We left within the day for Vaitupu, our last call in the Ellice Islands and, unlike Tarawa and Ocean, unravaged.

The yacht anchored six hundred yards off the reef to be surrounded by decorated canoes and singing islanders. Two girls sang the harmony and at the end of the chorus, time was beaten by the thump of each paddle on the sides of the canoes. Prince Philip embarked in the biggest canoe and was borne shoulder high in it across the beach to the celebrations. After an alofa (exchange of gifts) and native dancing the party adjourned for food to the maneaba, or meeting house.

The important guests were given roast sucking pig, bread-fruit and coconuts in large portions. When they had done their best the remains were handed on to the lesser guests. At a signal from a handsome Ellice maiden, sitting before each diner, the next course was brought in. Outside the maneaba a line of helpers slashed lumps of breadfruit and blackened sucking pig into manageable size before its journey on fresh palm leaves to the feast. The helpers kept up a brisk trotting pace and managed, by an occasional canter, to match supply with demand. Flies swarmed round the sunlit kitchen but those inside did not see them and those outside did not care.

The village was run by the London Mission Society; their Samoan pastor exercised a keen watch over their affairs. The pretty lagoon was used for swimming because the reef is infested with sharks. It was also used as the village lavatory; the huts perched on stilts over the blue water.

The libertymen from *Britannia* and *Rotoiti* who had braved the reef in a longboat were welcomed by the villagers and returned on board in a drenching rainstorm, with bartered mats, feather fans, baskets and yards of shell money. The yacht then laid off about four miles away, the admiral continued with his carpentry and Prince Philip went fishing in a sailing canoe.

The officers still ashore had a wet boat trip through a squall and a jump to the gangway in a four foot rise and fall of swell. It is forty years since I went to Vaitupu; it may now have been taken by tourism, but it was small and remote and had a chance. Our next island had none.

Christmas Island is 1716 miles from Vaitupu and half way across the Pacific. In 1959 it was an armed base and the headquarters for British atomic testing in the Pacific. Commissioned as HMS *Resolution*, saluting guns had been shipped specially from England to greet Prince Philip with a royal salute. It was normally uninhabited. Contract workers from the Gilbert and Ellice Islands had been brought in to provide the local labour. The British soldiers, sailors and airmen serving their one year tour 10,000 miles from home regarded our visit as the big event in their stay there. There were no white women and, except for superb opportunities for bird-watching and sea-fishing, the men enjoyed a similar life to those in Parkhurst, Dartmoor or Portland, without the excitement of an occasional conjugal visit.

We were given a display in their maneaba by the contract workers. The dancers sat in two lines waiting to begin. The wives too old for dancing lined one side of the meeting house with sleeping children on mats around them. The children did not wake. The music started with six men beating the top of a wooden packing case to an accompaniment from petrol tins and wooden sticks. The rhythm was deep and matched the haunting quality of the singing and the gestures of the women dancers. The noise grew louder and faster until, with a shout, it was over and the dancers sat down.

The last dance was the best, given by three girls dressed in several grass skirts (no Gilbertese would dance with only one) with flowers fastened to their hair, arms, ankles and between their fingers. They moved in perfect time to the beat of the music and songs of those sitting behind them. The music reached an ecstatic pitch, reflected in their eyes and flexing bodies. At the very end, when it seemed that someone in the audience might jump up and shout something, the three skirts gave a final shiver and the show

48

was over. These dances are a form of courtship display; the girls on Christmas Island danced among hundreds of lonely men and had become very good at it.

It was a fifteen day trip, the longest of the whole voyage, to cover the 4,764 miles to Balboa, Panama City and Colon, the Caribbean end of the canal, supported by the fourth and fifth replenishments at sea from RFA *Wave Vector*, and a mail drop by a Hastings aircraft from Christmas Island. A Phoenix petrel with a damaged left eye sat at the back of the bridge and took off the day before we saw South America. He guessed correctly that it was his last chance to fly south to the plankton while he had the strength to get there.

Panama City was in turmoil, all neon signs, rowdy streets and litter. The ambassador had sent a warning signal that our visit might have to be cancelled because of political trouble. Flashy American cars cruised up and down the main street, filled with men looking for diversions. The yachtsmen were never slow to find a phrase and called it Vizag on wheels. Revolution, led by the husband of Margot Fonteyn, the British ballerina, hovered.

A reception was held on a poorly lit tennis court at the embassy. The British officials expected trouble. One of them told me that government ministers could make six million dollars a year and there were plenty of volunteers for the jobs. I was interviewed in the gloom by an American journalist for the local radio station. I kept the nugget about the cabinet ministers prospects to myself.

The ship was towed through the canal by six tractors (called mules) in a smart operation by the canal company. At Colon the US governor of the Canal Zone entertained Prince Philip and seven from the wardroom. We found silver punch bowls, lace tablecloths, stewards in white gloves, coloured sandwiches, Californian strawberries and women in smart clothes. The dark embassy tennis court was another world.

That evening we left for the Bahamas and more civilisation,

49

passing through the Crooked Island Passage on the 23rd April before anchoring off Conception Island, among the cays where buccaneers careened their ships and buried their treasure. The white sand was sunlit a cricket pitch's length beneath our hull.

Nassau, when I saw it, was a heavily capitalised Weston-super-Mare, geared to American packaged tourism. It operated a toe-curling display of its connection to the British Empire, with guards, flags, soldiers and government house. The yacht's senior officers were able to escape to a fully staffed comfortable house generously lent by an absent Earl of Dudley.

On 28th April we arrived in Bermuda to oil and foresook white uniform. Nigel and I were bidden to a dinner of the Association of Royal Navy Officers and I found there two officers I knew from Italy in 1944-45 – Colonel Sankey, the commander of 42 RM Commando at Lake Commachio, and Commander Kitson, the admiral's secretary at Taranto. Sankey had two black labrador dogs who reminded me of my Jake.

'Pity they can never get any shooting here.'

'They are superb guard dogs though.'

'Not usual for labradors?'

'These chaps are hopelessly racially prejudiced.'

Prince Philip and the household party left to fly home. John, one of the junior lieutenants, arrived on board in the early hours to be told that the navigating officer had gone with the royal party and we were off across the Atlantic as soon as the boats were hoisted. He was the assistant navigator and had inherited the top job. He had no difficulty and it seemed a short haul before the Needles were once more on the beam, this time on the starboard side.

Plate 5: 17 March 1959 – Crossing the Line; Julie and the Bears

Plate 6: 19 March 1959, Savo Island from Honiara, Solomon Islands. Three Allied heavy cruisers were sunk in a night action in the channel here on 9 August 1942

Plate 7: 19 March 1959 – Honiara, Solomon Islands;
Brownies on parade

Plate 8: March 1959 – Pacific; Don and Rodney

Plate 9: 28 March 1959, Ocean Island: SS Kelvinbank *on the reef*

Plate 10: 30 March 1959, HRH The Duke of Edinburgh landing at Vaitupu, Ellice Island

Plate 11: 19 March 1959, Graciosa Bay, Solomon Islands; the pipe had a silver band from somewhere

Plate 12: 1 April 1959, Christmas Island dancers

Chapter 4

THE OPENING OF THE ST LAWRENCE SEAWAY – 1959

THE QUEEN EMBARKED IN THE YACHT in five out of the ten cruises in my time; the opening of the Seaway in 1959 was the first. We left Portsmouth on 6th June 1959 to be in Canada when she arrived there. The previous eight months were a curtain-raiser. This time *Britannia* would be in her primary role.

The ship went astern briskly from North Corner Jetty with the wind, aiming to turn in the middle of the harbour and point for the entrance. On the bridge we watched the dockyard receding before us but no one seems to have looked aft until the yeoman shouted a warning. Our course was taking us into the middle of a cruiser in reserve, moored bow and stern to buoys at right angles to our approach and getting rapidly closer. The engine room artificers on the telegraphs, with their usual dexterity, went from half astern to full ahead before a thump on our delicate behind put us back alongside, probably for some time. Entering and leaving harbour continued to thrill.

Diary 7th June, 1959 – Portsmouth to Sydney, Nova Scotia

Bumpy night south of the Irish Sea and a monstrous swell, right in our path, in the morning. Ship standing on her head. Admiral told me he is getting another job after the yacht.

Diary 12th June, 1959

Off Grand Banks. Easterly gale. Rain, mist, fog and an ice warning. Ship stopped at midnight in the fog. At daylight the fog began clearing. Admiral recalled similar passage in SS Empress of Britain *with the King and Queen in 1939. Passed within a cable of three icebergs surrounded by all kinds of sea birds.*

We arrived at Sydney, Nova Scotia, at the entrance to the Gulf of St Lawrence, 24 hours late because of the unbroken gales on passage. This was a convenient place to clean up before *Britannia's* shiny hull met the concrete locks in the St Lawrence. The dockyard had fitted elm rubbing strakes beneath the water line. They ought to work. That sort of device worked on yachts transiting the French canals. It was not much of a precedent but there were few precedents for this voyage.

A petty officer of the Women's Royal Canadian Naval Service joined as assistant to the acting royal press secretary. She must have been the first woman naval rating to join the seagoing complement of one of HM ships. Two officers and fifteen ratings of the RCN had already arrived; the Queen would be on board as Queen of Canada and the Canadian national flag would later take the place of the Union Flag at our mizzen mast. The two days at Sydney introduced us to the paparazzi of the New World, tigers compared to the pussy cats at home. They approached our hierarchical world with relish. The admiral had enjoyed modest success on the local television. Immediately afterwards I was telephoned by a producer offering him £100 for a half hour appearance on a New York equivalent of *What's My Line*, plus free air travel and accommodation.

A local pressman wanted his photograph. 'Say, who am I getting here. Is it the captain of the boat?' – It was the supply officer of the RCN base.

The welcome was genuine, particularly from the Canadian navy, and made up for the ironworks, dirty frame houses, broken roads and scrub vegetation. Only three yachtsmen went ashore.

Diary 16th June, 1959 – Sydney to Sept Iles

At 1800 General Graham (Governor-General) rang from Newfoundland to say that we should go to Sept Iles twenty-four hours earlier in case the Queen's aircraft could not land in Newfoundland on Thursday. Further bombshell – Canadian government wants to seal all refrigerators (including the ones used by the royal party) at Montreal before we go on west, in compliance with a foot and mouth disease ordinance. We can't have that.

17th June

Sent for in morning watch. Admiral had a sleepless night about this refrigerator business and wants a meeting at 0800. After the meeting he rang General Graham at 0900 who agreed that something would be done.

Sept Iles, on the northern side of the St Lawrence is the rail and sea head for the Labrador ore mines 500 miles up-country. It lives by minerals, which cover the district with dust. The yacht went alongside behind an ore carrier loading at 8000 tons per hour; our upper deck was smothered at once with a red film. The local fire chief sent an engine to wash down the starboard side before the Queen arrived, when the royal standard was broken at the mainmast and the tour began. We left at once for Gaspe, reversing course to the other side of the estuary, with an escort of two Canadian and one British destroyers. At 0400 the fog closed down and the rest of the night was made hideous by the siren.

Gaspe Bay provided the right setting and space for a naval

review by the Queen of 18 ships of the British and Canadian navies. The RN provided a destroyer and two submarines. *Britannia* cruised down the line, the ship's companies cheered and the new Canadian frigates, all post war, stuffed with equipment, made the old RN WW II destroyer not only look battle hardened, which she was, but battle weary.

When we left Gaspe the introductory part of the cruise was over. So far, in terms of geography at home, we had been sent to the likes of Barry, Avonmouth and Tor Bay. Port Alfred and the Saguenay River sounded better.

The river is deep and navigable, running between high cliffs. The scent of the larch, spruce and pine trees clinging to the walls enveloped us. Port Alfred is a small French Canadian settlement with a pulp mill and a giant log pond. Twenty miles away at Avida the biggest aluminium smelting plant in the world ensures the town's place on the economic map.

The stay there was short. That evening, on passage to Quebec, the new officers were presented to the Queen. I had seen her from time to time in Malta when she was a naval wife. Any confidence that I might have derived from that soon vanished. When face to face with the sovereign for the first time I found something in my genes made ready answers hard to find.

Our first heaving line landed at Quebec at the exact programmed arrival time, after an immaculate alongside by the admiral in awkward conditions. On the jetty a royal guard of the 22me Regiment in scarlet and bearskin paraded to orders in French before a large crowd of onlookers. 1959 was the two hundredth anniversary of Wolf's victory on the Plains of Abraham.

St Jean Batiste, the patron saint of French Canada, had his saint's day about this time and holidays had started. The Quebecois had a good excuse for turning out for the royal visit without compromising the loyalty they owed to their ancestors, who had colonised Upper Canada and fought the British to the death. The arrangements had been tactfully planned.

Five of us made the pilgrimage to the battlefield. The plains are crossed by a metalled road and the Chateau Frontegnac Hotel hangs on the skyline. The cliffs have not been disfigured. Quebec was the greatest of all the victories in 1759, the *annus mirabilis*, described by Fortescue:

> *– this most delicate and critical operation was so admirably thought out and executed by the officers of both services that it must abide for ever a masterpiece in its kind. The British navy and army working, as at Quebec, in concord and harmony under loyal and able chiefs, are indeed not easily baffled.*

Two hundred years later, *Britannia's* officers were not required to bear arms; they were mustered to entertain the press.

Diary 23rd June, 1959 – at Quebec

Attended a press reception on board for 500, although I do not think that 500 turned up. All officers were there to deal with them. Talked to Stacey of Daily Express, *Anne Sharpley of* Evening Standard, Time and Tide *chap and an American from a Detroit paper. Had an argument with Tom Stacey about Beaverbrook. A woman called June Smallwood has written a scurrilous piece in the American magazine* Look. *The story goes that she was presented to the Queen at this party and was seen in tears later, overcome by conscience.*

At 0230 next morning the yacht left for a short stop at Trois Rivières, the newsprint centre of the world, surrounded by log mountains. Here Prince Philip took her alongside and touched the paint on the starboard quarter, a trivial episode, gobbled up by the press.

The afternoon cruise up river was made through an armada of fast speed boats, waving crowds and decorated tugs. Alongside in

Montreal the yachtsmen had two days to polish her, repair the hull damage caused by an oiler, and generally get braced up for the aim of the tour, Seaway Day One.

Diary 26th June, 1959 – at Montreal

The big day. Prime Minister Diefenbaker of Canada arrived twenty minutes early. The Queen met President Eisenhower at the airfield while we moved to a special jetty at the entrance to the Seaway, the site for the opening ceremony. The tide was pushing us against our berth and the admiral took tugs. The forward tug snapped one of our new wires and we had an awkward job getting off. The yacht went under the Jacques Cartier bridge and secured to two large pontoons constituting the special jetty. As she went under the span the top twenty feet of her mainmast bent backwards on the hinge which had been fitted for the cruise. The aerial on the foremast bent forwards. The process was called 'scandalising' and it was repeated six times during the day as the bridges were passed.
Each time, the royal standard and the president's flag, when he was on board, were transferred to the foremast in place of the Lord High Admiral's flag. At the St Lambert Lock the ship scandalised, dressed ship and locked in at the same time, involving everyone on the upper deck in a symphony of movement when any error would have been obvious.
In the absence of the Queen's Press Secretary I was given eighteen paparazzi to look after. They were not allowed off the upper deck and peered through the curtains in the drawing room and dining room. They were cheered up with copies of the menu.
The Queen embarked with President Eisenhower after the opening ceremonies and went to the royal bridge. Fifty royal guests were taken to the royal deck. The yacht headed for the first lock.

The dressing lines and their flags are substantial and come down with a rush. I suggested to Christian Herter, the American Secretary of State, that it might be prudent to move in case they landed where he was sitting. He thanked me courteously and stayed where he was. Being somewhat disabled, he was probably fed up with well-meaning idiots giving him advice.

Buffet lunch in the charthouse for my party. One of the pressmen made a speech of thanks, to the amusement of the wardroom, there to help me out. They called on me to reply. Nothing doing.

The yacht went through the ceremonial gateway to the Seaway with an international destroyer escort of HMS *Ulster*, HMCS *Gatineau* and USS *Forrest Sherman* in line astern. The Seaway was officially open. Now came the new locks. In planning for the cruise the navigating officer had flown to inspect them twice and the admiral once. We knew what to expect.

There were about twelve and a half feet each side to play with. Our hull shimmered with blue gloss paint and the gold leaf line. She was an unlikely ship to take through a series of these concrete boxes. Any seaman knows about canal effect and the difficulty of handling a ship in a lock being flooded at speed. It was thus with interest that the forecastle hands of *Britannia* looked at the chasm of the St Lambert opening up ahead, lined with cheering crowds, while their sovereign watched the proceedings from the royal bridge behind them.

She settled into the lock, the six wires were made fast, the gates closed and she rose smoothly and quickly with the flood. Later on there were two occasions when she lost a little paint and the jolly boat in davits was rubbed, but she behaved very well on this and the thirty-one other lockings which followed.

The yachtsmen dressed ship and undressed ship, locked and unlocked, scandalised and rehoisted as the hot day went by, while the crowds waved and cheered, the small boats buzzed about and *Britannia* slid on through the Seaway, a famous ship on perhaps her greatest day.

In Lake St Louis sixteen Canadian and US warships cheered as the royal squadron steamed closely down their line. The last ship was the big missile cruiser USS *Macon* with two jumbo Regulus missiles dangling over her stern. She had arrived so that she would be able to leave but there seemed to be a great deal of her for comfort.

The President and his party disembarked while the yacht waited in the Lower Beauharnois Lock for three helicopters to carry them away in a cloud of dust. After one more lock and two more bridges *Britannia* came to a buoy at eight o'clock that evening in Couteau anchorage. Seaway Day One was over.

Seaway Day Two was a reminder of what could have happened on the opening day. The French Canadian pilots struck over their contracts and the canal was buried in fog.

The first problem was solved, the second made us two hours late in leaving. She groped her way ahead behind one of her boats with the assistant navigating officer embarked. The ship fixed on the boat by radar, anchoring twice when it was impossible to move. The decision to appoint a second navigating officer for this cruise had paid off.

Britannia arrived in Snell Lock, New York State, five hours late. The Queen disembarked there and carried out an alternative programme, returning later when we had reached the Iroquois Lock. In that time she had opened, in company with Vice-President Nixon, the Moses-Saunders River Power Dam. The westward passage through the Seaway ended at Brockville where we anchored at 8.45 pm that day. The admiral put up a notice:

By command of Her Majesty The Queen, the mainbrace will be spliced in *Britannia* tomorrow, Sunday. Her Majesty is aware of the hard work which has been done during the past two days.

We were all aware too of the hard work that the Queen had done and the inspiration she had been to *Britannia's* crew, whose philosophy was simple; the best was required and they had given it.

We left the concrete of the Seaway without regret to cruise the St Lawrence on a summer day through the Thousand Islands archipelago, surrounded again by small boats. Each island is the summer home of a prosperous American or Canadian, with trees, lawns and a jetty. Two months before, these delights would have been covered in ice and snow.

At midday the wardroom spliced the mainbrace and drank dark brown rum cocktails provided gratis through the Navy Vote. The household were invited and there was a rumour that the Queen might visit us. We changed rapidly into long white uniform. Prince Philip arrived and announced that the Queen would not be coming; she was having her hair done.

That afternoon the ship anchored off the Canadian cadet training college at Kingston. On the bridge the admiral dropped the anchor flag, the fo'c'stle party knocked the slip off the cable, the anchor hit the water and the onlookers waited to see the dressing lines covered with flags rise to the three mastheads, propelled upwards as usual by the muscles of the Supply Division. Nothing happened. Seconds later the flags rose slowly and then accelerated as more hands arrived to take the strain. The admiral was annoyed. It would have been bad enough anywhere; it was a humiliation in front of a military school.

A senior officer announced publicly that the Supply Division had let the side down and I knew that it could not be true. My deputy, Hugh, was on the upper deck in charge of the hoist. He reported to me that his party had not been released from their entering harbour stations in time to man the dressing lines before the anchor was let go. He was a quiet and utterly dependable officer and said that his men were being blamed without cause. I told the senior officer concerned that I intended to report to the admiral what my deputy had said and asked him to be there when I did so. He refused and I saw the admiral alone. I told Hugh to tell the hands what had happened.

I set down this tale of a typical snarl up of a kind that happens sometimes on the upper decks of Her Majesty's ships to illustrate how differently these things were seen in *Britannia*. There failure was hard to take. When mistakes were made straightforward people found it difficult to accept it. All this increased the tension, particularly on a major cruise and emphasised the need for senior officers with perspective and a sense of humour. I hasten to confess that at Kingston I was in danger of losing both.

Britannia and her three escorts passed down a line of representative merchant ships and entered the Western Approach entrance to Toronto harbour with the sun reflecting the yacht's sides on the still water of the lake. The squadron gave the locals a dramatic reminder of their new ocean link.

We had become used to being in the news but the interest we raised here was extraordinary. The jetty was thronged with thousands of sightseers hoping to see the Queen. Football stands put there were rarely less than half full and broadcast music entertained the spectators when no early appearance of the Queen could be expected. Royal yachtsmen going ashore were often mobbed by well-wishers.

The Queen did not disappoint them. When she left to attend a dinner dressed in ermine and Garter, tiara and diamonds, she travelled with an interior light in her car. The crowds went mad.

For two days we became a focus for the many living in Toronto with British roots. A Canadian reserve officer I had served with in the Halifax escort force arrived on board with his wife and three children to say hello. The Professor of Anatomy at Toronto University who had been a young doctor in the same ship followed. The yacht's soccer team drew with a police eleven and received twenty minutes on prime television and eleven engraved tankards.

The Queen disembarked before we began the transit of the eight old locks of the Welland Canal system, enabling ships to travel from Lake Ontario to Lake Erie. It was Dominion Day and the weather was warm.

Diary 1st July, 1959 – Toronto to Windsor

. . . transited the eight locks of the Welland system. Sides lined with people for the whole thirty miles – cars everywhere, union flags and smiling faces, all delighted to see us. Some of the old people overcome. The most moving welcome we have had in Canada. The locks are not new but we got through without damage. Turbulence strong but the elm rubbing strakes help to take the bumps. On clearing Port Colborne and entering Lake Erie we met one of the famous Great Lake squalls. Water black and wrinkled, whistling wind and rain. The lake's ships are remarkable sights – all hulls with tiny bows and sterns.

The yacht entered the Detroit River, passed by the Ford Rouge River plant and under the Ambassador Bridge, linking Canada and the USA, to an alongside berth at Windsor, on the Canadian side.

Over the river, the skyline was filled by the skyscrapers of Detroit, a monument to western capitalism. On our side, the modest town of Windsor was a poor relation, probably used to fetching and carrying for its giant neighbour. On this occasion the presence of *Britannia*, albeit temporarily without the Queen embarked, ensured that Windsor took the honours.

Two of us visited the maelstrom of Detroit and found crowds on the riverside there watching the yacht. The city exists in an apparent fever of activity, its citizens on foot constantly marshalled by flashing lights telling them to 'Walk!' or 'Don't Walk!' thus avoiding the racing chequered cabs. The men seemed to favour straw hats, tie pins and good shoes. The city was crossed by a broad noble main street. In the centre we found an air force display with the most decorated B29 bomber of World War Two, bracketed by Nike and Atlas missiles. Provincial Windsor was more like home.

The Queen re-embarked after her tour of Ontario to an ecstatic welcome from a great crowd on shore. Both banks of the wide river were lined with people when we left that evening.

The journey up the Detroit River and through Lake St Clair was the usual holiday procession which our voyage through the Middle West had become. US coastguards in fast motor boats and helicopters kept the speed boats around us clear, while on shore the thick green lawns before the American riverside homes were planted with flags and lined with waving members of the family. Some fired starting guns; occasionally the view was blocked by the hull of a Great Lakes freighter, a warehouse on water, passing on opposite course with siren hooting and ensign at the dip.

In Lake Huron the Queen left to travel by train to Parry Sound, at the north-eastern end of the lake. While we waited there for her to return, among the usual flotillas of small boats, a seaplane circled the anchorage and landed off our starboard quarter. It then taxied through the boats until it was a hundred yards or so off our beam, when the engine was switched off. A grey-headed pilot climbed stiffly and slowly on to the floats with a packet of sandwiches, which he ate with deliberation while inspecting us. The sandwiches gone he found his way back to the cockpit and took off.

On Sunday 4th July, with three US and two RCN destroyers and *Ulster*, and the royal standard at the main, the squadron cruised Lakes Huron and Michigan to Chicago. Beneath the enormous Mackinack Bridge at the entrance to Lake Michigan a battery fired a royal salute as we passed under the sweeping cables and piers, half hidden by fog.

The Queen was the first reigning monarch to visit Chicago, then the eighth largest city in the world, two thousand miles from the sea and so unaware of the distant oceans that they have only one word for ship. Everything is a 'boat', in the language of lakes, rivers and ponds. They may think small in maritime matters but they think very big about everything else, as they soon made clear.

As we entered the harbour to a specially dredged berth at a buoy, we were met by coloured fountains ashore and afloat, gun salutes, sirens and cheering spectators. When the Queen landed she stepped on to a 100 feet red carpet leading to the four-service guard of honour and streets lined with two million people waiting for the motorcade. Overhead a wing of seventy fighters and bombers dipped in salute. They were not in the programme but the USAAF general commanding them decided that he wanted his boys to be there.

The admiral had been asked to appear on the local media and told me to take his place. On the jetty I looked in vain for Jack Boswell the Canadian Broadcasting Corporation man who had set it up. I approached two policemen of unusual size who seemed to be armed to Panzer Grenadier scale.

'Excuse me officer, could you please direct me to the local television station?'

'Which one? We got four.'

Jack arrived; we found the studio and were taken to meet Miss Lee Philips, the hostess of the programme in which I was to appear. Miss Philips ran a fifteen minute daily show for women entitled *Shopping with Miss Lee* which was popular in Chicago. I came on after the 'Angel Food' commercial and answered Miss Lee's questions about *Britannia* while the camera kept returning to my cap, on a table between us. It was my best uniform cap and, so far as the director was concerned, the important part of the show. I was followed by two young British doctors, on an exchange tour at a Chicago hospital. The show that day concentrated on the UK and tried to draw the attention of the six million living in the great 'wen' on the prairie to some islands five thousand miles away that few of them would ever see and most seldom think about.

The exodus from *Britannia* to shore that day was total and the ship was left to the care of the duty part of the watch while the rest examined Chicago.

The three commanding officers of the US destroyers arrived on board in mid-afternoon, as requested by the household, to be presented with signed photographs of the Queen to commemorate their escort duty. They were taken to the wardroom while a messenger went aft to report their arrival. The household, like the rest of us not on duty, were ashore. No one else knew anything about it. The officer of the day worked hard to entertain the three Americans while someone sought out my chief writer who rarely went ashore and had a good liaison with the household clerical staff. He was run down under a shower. It was nothing to do with him but by some chance he remembered where the household kept the photographs and found the key. The problem was half solved. The photographs were there, already signed. All that was needed was a donor. The senior yacht officer on board could not do it, being junior to the Americans, still waiting patiently for some action. The admiral came back at that moment and the Americans got their rewards.

The Queen returned at midnight after a thirteen hour day. The royal squadron left at once for the passage through Lakes Michigan and Superior to Port Arthur, the most westerly navigable place in Canada, where the yacht would turn round for home.

Diary 7th July, 1959 – Chicago to Sault Ste Marie, Port Arthur and Hamilton

Closed Milwaukee on passage north at 0830 so that the locals could see the Royal Squadron. Met Prince Philip on the bridge

ladder.
'Good morning, sir.'
'Good morning. We admired your performance on the television yesterday.'
They must have watched it in their hotel before lunch. Glad I did not know.

At the entrance to Lake Superior the squadron used the down channel because the American destroyers drew too much water to use the up channel. The yacht had to move to the Canadian side and lock through in a cross wind, a difficult operation which the admiral did well, losing a little paint only.

When the squadron left Sault St Marie that evening for Port Arthur the commanding officers of the remaining Canadian and British escorts were bidden to dinner with the Queen. They gathered in one ship to simplify the transfer at sea by high line. Fog descended, the operation became dangerous and the dinner was abandoned. The commanding officers had to stay where they were.

Fort William and Port Arthur adjoin and together constitute Thunder Bay but do not always see eye to eye. The mayor of Port Arthur had asked the royal squadron to enter by the Port Arthur entrance, cruise along the inside of the breakwater and leave by the Fort William entrance before anchoring outside the harbour. *Britannia* led the squadron in while locals from both communities gathered on the shore to watch the show. We could see the masts of many small boats over the top of the breakwater, covered with flags and manned by enthusiastic spectators. The yacht passed the entrance and turned to starboard, expecting the boats to get out of her way. As we got closer it became clear that they were all at anchor and unable to move in a hurry. No one had told them what was going on, meanwhile *Britannia* and three destroyers were bearing down at seven knots with no time to alter course. The squadron went astern smartly and no damage was done.

The three commanding officers of the escort were sent for to be thanked personally by the Queen for their services and given signed photographs. The captain of HMS *Ulster* was still on board the Canadian *Kootenay* where he had gone the night before to be transferred for the cancelled dinner. The fog and the operational programme had not enabled him to get back to his ship. Special dispensation was given for him to come to *Britannia* in the white mess undress which he had put on eighteen hours before.

The royal standard was struck and the Queen left to continue her tour of Western Canada. It would not be re-hoisted until she re-embarked at New Brunswick at the end of the visit.

The squadron had twenty-four hours to explore the log ponds and grain elevators at the lakehead, where the twin mountains of an Indian reservation show to the south and ships are 600 feet above sea level and two thousand miles from the Atlantic. These waters had not been visited by the Royal Navy since the war of 1812.

Fourteen officers from each ship of the squadron attended a dinner given by the civic dignitaries of Port Arthur and Fort William. Fort William was represented by their mayor, a large Italian lady of evident character and resolution. Over two hundred attended and she was the only lady there.

At precisely 7.30pm the dinner and speeches ended. The president announced, 'These festivities are now over and would you all please leave.' I am afraid that it was an invitation that our contingent were glad to accept, if only to escape the white wine, served in bottles hidden in napkins. I turned to my neighbour,

'What do you think it is?'

'Petrol.'

'Incredible.'

'Four star, though. This is a special night.'

This sounds unkind but they did not seem keen to see us. The local press claimed on its front page that we had entered harbour too quickly, been unable to turn in time and had gone aground.

The yacht now reversed her course for home and found that even without the royal standard she had become a Canadian attraction. In the locks of the Welland Canal we were met by solid crowds with shouts of welcome and cries for the band, which were always answered. During the sudden quiet as the lock gates opened and we slid out we heard the voice of an old lady perched fifty feet above us:

'God bless each and every one of you!'

From an old-timer – 'Any engine room there? I was chief ERA of *Valiant.*'

Answered at once (and truthfully) by a voice from our waist:

'Yes, here. I was chief ERA of *Queen Elizabeth.*'

Sometimes there was no answer to be made, when the crowd sang *Land of Hope and Glory* and shouted things that had not been heard for a generation. They knew about the future of the empire now; many of them were probably first generation Canadians from the UK. The great days were nearly over; *Britannia*, for a short time, brought them back.

Hamilton is a steel making city on Lake Ontario with a history from the old wars and a strong pro-British leaning. Niagara and Buffalo are within reach. The hospitality shown to us was unbounded. A telephone call asking two yachtsmen to a dinner invitation had to be refused because there was no one left not on duty.

Sometimes there were advantages in staying on board.

Letter to my wife, 17 July, 1959 – Hamilton

We were all given a basket of cherries by the mayor at Hamilton. Everyone has been wonderfully kind to us. Dining aft this evening with Mark Milbank, the admiral and Geoff Cornish. Mark is the only member of the household still here.

71

We dine in solitary state.

On Saturday, 18th July, the yacht passed through the Upper Beauharnois, Lower Beauharnois, St Catherine and St Lambert locks, the twenty-ninth, thirtieth, thirty-first and thirty-second of her cruise, and went alongside at Victoria Basin, Montreal. The temperature and humidity were formidable. The locals go to the Laurentian Mountains to escape.

We were six days in Montreal, the longest stay anywhere abroad, except Vizagapatam, since the yacht left Portsmouth in January. The hospitality cascaded over us; again, it was usually the duty part of the watch only who were obliged to sweat it out on board.

A joint calling party of the admiral, commander, doctor and I visited the French Canadian mayor. Lady Angela Dawnay, who was with the admiral in Montreal, came too. The mayor had been in post for some time and was assisted by his brother, who was his secretary and chief of staff. We were given sherry and an ash tray each and a tour of the council chamber. The mayor was friendly and charming. His great city is only smaller than Paris among the cities of the world where French is spoken. Compared with Toronto, Halifax or Hamilton, Montreal seemed abroad.

We were told that the Queen would not be coming back across the Atlantic with us as planned. No reason was given and we left Montreal for two days fresh air at the Quebec resort of Murray Bay, before the Queen embarked at Shediac in New Brunswick for the short passage to Charlottetown on Prince Edward Island, where she would leave the yacht to fly home from Halifax.

The departure from Montreal needed a display of faith in the pilot. The yacht's bows were pointing upstream so that she had to be turned round before going down river. We left the jetty stern first, sheltered from the current by another jetty. As soon as there was room, and before meeting the full force of the stream, her bows were turned into the flow. Nothing happened and for a moment all eyes were upon the pilot. Then the river caught her and spun her round like a top. She was on her way down river before the pilot could light his cigarette and say 'OK.'

At Murray Bay we anchored at 0330 in deep water. As the cable was paid out a defective link broke and the anchor and seven and a half shackles of cable went to the sandy bottom 120 feet below. The yacht was secured in a hurry by the starboard anchor.

The regulations demand that ships unfortunate enough to lose an anchor must use every muscle to find it. Thus for the next two days, with help from RCN divers flown from Halifax, *Britannia's* crew worked hard in open boats dragging, buoying and fixing in rough conditions of wind and tide in attempts to find the missing gear. They were beaten by the tide and a thirty knot blow, which lasted the whole time we were there. *Ulster* provided a dan buoy to mark the spot and we had to leave with only one anchor.

At Shediac in New Brunswick we were clear of the great river and met three waiting RCN destroyers of the royal escort. The Queen embarked at 1830 and the squadron sailed at 0230 for Charlottetown where she left for the last time on the cruise. The yacht went to Halifax.

Diary 31st July and 1st August, 1959 – Shediac to Halifax

Arrived Halifax in thick fog which lifted enough to pass down a line of RCN ships on north side of the harbour. The fog closed in on the port side and we went very close to a fishing boat, causing a boy to jump over in fright. Berthed in the dockyard, astern of the RCN carrier Bonaventure.

On a green bank under the admiral's office 'H.M.C. Dockyard 1759' picked out in white stones. Borrowed a port anchor from the yard.

1st August, 1959

Attended presentation of a new colour by the Queen to the R.C.N. at the Garrison Grounds. Bluejacket band very good.

73

Delightful ceremony after dusk when the Queen drove down and embarked in her barge astern of us. We manned the after end, the bluejacket band played 'Will Ye No Come Back Again' and a choir sang. The crowd on the bank cheered as she went down our starboard side. The Queen could be seen clearly under the cabin light of the barge which went under the long string of the suspension bridge, past the illuminated warships to the air station and the Comet waiting to take her to London. We sailed as soon as the boats were hoisted although we have not been told where we are going. Admiralty informed we intend to meet oiler off Rockall.

On the 7th August we met our oiler RFA *Wave Chief*. On the same day we learned that the yacht was going to Portsmouth and would be reducing to harbour complement. The cruises to Scotland and West Africa that were planned for the rest of the year were cancelled. The Queen was expecting a baby in the new year.

We went up-channel and dined out the six officers who were leaving, as was the custom. As was the custom too, the senior officers assembled in Chief's cabin the night before Portsmouth, to discuss the cruise, what was needed next time and what was wrong with the navy. The meeting was known as 'Channel Night' and as usual it went on too long and too much noise was made. This time we were admonished in writing. There was no excuse of course. At our ages and seniorities if we felt we had to let off steam we should not have been there at all.

Plate 13: 13 June 1959, Quebec

Plate 14: 26 June 1959, Seaway Day One

Plate 15: 26 June 1959, Seaway Day One – St Lambert Lock

Plate 16: 2 July 1959, Windsor, Ontario – Detroit in the background

Plate 17: 2 July 1959: Visit to Windsor Daily Star. RCN liaison officer on left

Plate 18: 3 July 1959; departure from Windsor

Plate 19: 22 July 1959; Calling party on the Mayor of Montreal

Chapter 5

CRUISE OF HRH THE PRINCESS ROYAL
TO THE WEST INDIES – 1960

THE YACHT VISITED TWENTY-TWO PLACES and gave the West Indies a good looking over, in this, her first cruise in 1960. The ship wore the standard of Princess Mary, HRH The Princess Royal, the only daughter of King George the Fifth, a royal lady who had shewn an early interest in *Britannia*. In 1954, the year the ship was commissioned, the Princess embarked for an eight mile voyage from Cowes to Portsmouth. Born in 1897, she provided a rare link between *Britannia* and its predecessor, *Victoria and Albert III*.

On the 15th January 1960, we left the ice and slush of Portsmouth and headed past the Needles towards the sunshine for the fifth time in twelve months.

Diary 17th January, 1960 – Portsmouth to Georgetown

Force 6 from south by 1600. Went aft for drinks with HRH's household untroubled by the weather – Vice-Admiral Sir Geoffrey and Lady Margaret Hawkins and Major Eastwood.

19th January, 1960

Passed Azores during the night and now in about 37 degrees N

– near the spot where the German barque Pamir *was lost with all hands not long ago. Fifty feet of manilla rope, together with the drum and other gear disappeared from the fo'c'stle. No one saw it go. Number One, boatswain and two sailors were swamped by a sea when trying to secure remaining drum. Sailors cut and bruised. All four could easily have gone the way of the lost manilla.*

20th January, 1960

Now gusting Force 9-10 from S. Down to 9 knots.

21st January, 1960

Now Force 3-4. Increased to 17 Knots. Did storeroom rounds and began blitz on main naval store which needed it.

22nd January, 1960

Sunshine! Tropical rig.

RFA *Brown Ranger* met us in mid-Atlantic after a fourteen day voyage from Malta, where she was based with her Maltese crew. We did our best to cheer up the master in the charthouse while the refuelling went on. He described his ship as '*Britannia's* tanker' but he had no orders, no mail, no money to pay his hands and no one loved him.

The admiral cleared lower deck and told the yachtsmen that he had no idea of the summer programme but he thought it would be a quiet one and time for leave when we went back to Portsmouth. The dates for summer leave were announced. This was unfortunate. The lesson learned was that our programme could never be foreseen with certainty. Despite our size and complement we were in the private yachting business and dependant upon royal

81

family plans and holidays, as well as the cruises fixed long ahead where matters of state were directly involved.

At dinner I sat next to the princess; the naval specialist surgeon, who joined when members of the royal family were there, sat the other side. The doctor engrossed her about natural history cycles. Lady Margaret Hawkins, on my right, said that she had shot a lion. I had no contribution to offer to this conversation save the story of a bullock we shot on the trackers' advice during a night shoot for leopard. I decided to keep that one to myself.

After dinner HRH began her *gros point* while Admiral Hawkins talked to me about Malta and the day he inspected *Phoenicia*. I was first lieutenant there at that time and borrowed a bugler from the Highland Light Infantry to beef up the ceremony. He stood on top of the curtain wall in his full highland gear and sounded the alert as the barge came alongside the jetty at Fort Manuel.

The admiral said that for a moment he had not been sure whether it was cheeky or enterprising.

While the surgeon and I were doing our best to sing for our supper our admiral, unintentionally I am sure, gave the impression he sometimes gave when royals were about that he was at home and we were having a treat. It was usually true anyway.

The princess, her lady-in-waiting and Lady Margaret called on the wardroom next day. During Lady Margaret's time in Malta her two daughters volunteered for a chorus line of belly-dancers in an amateur concert. One of them was so good at it that when her mother saw the rehearsal she ordered all the girls to cover their tummies for the show. This concern with decorum did not indicate a lack of a sense of humour. She told me that she had taken to wearing low heels because she had to do so much standing on royal duty that her feet were killing her, particularly when the ship was in a seaway. She added that the royal family could stand for hours because their muscles had got used to it.

After a fourteen day voyage, while still twenty miles from land, the sea went brown from the waters of the Demerara River. The survey ship, HMS *Vidal*, which was yawing about at anchor at the mouth of the estuary, fired a gun salute and manned ship to cheer as we passed up the muddy water to Georgetown, the capital of British Guiana, a modest colony in the imperial collection. The yacht was ten minutes late after a poor turn into the current and wind caused a near miss on an anchored ferry

At that time the Booker company, centred on rum and sugar, was a major employer there. The town might have been laid out by a Victorian engineer, working to a familiar design. The roads were wide and straight and the houses built in the same pleasing colonial style with balconies, shutters and verandahs.

Cricket was an obsession in British Guiana. We were soon taken to the ground where Len Hutton had marched the MCC off to avoid flying bottles. Apparently the trouble that day came from lost bets.

The Botanical Gardens had a mixture of vivid toucans and parrots and hideous snakes and tapirs. This was South America.

Our cricket side was beaten by Bookers by 200 runs in a one day match. I put myself on the boundary and watched two go over my head on to the road. I caught the third and as the batsman walked out I saw the the royal motorcade approaching. I called the side to attention and to remove headgear. Admiral Hawkins gave us a friendly wave; the opposition thought that we were calling up divine help. Undoubtedly that would have been our best bet. It helped for a moment to take our lads' minds off the thrashing we were getting.

After four days at Georgetown we left for Port of Spain, Trinidad, 400 miles to the north. Today, forty years on, I most remember HMS *Vidal*, far from home in the grubby Demerara estuary, and the chief of police there, a young man barely thirty-five who had been captured by the Japanese while with the infantry in Burma.

His wife wanted to go to the Trinidad carnival. She announced to the party at a dance that if he would not take her she would find someone who would. This would have been no problem for her unless her husband was prepared to shut her in the cooler until the carnival was over.

The princess disembarked during our four day visit to Port of Spain and stayed with Lord Hailes, the governor-general of the West Indies under a recent re-organisation. He had taken over the governor's house when he arrived there. Hailes was a politician and Sir Edward Beetham, the governor, a colonial civil servant who resented having to move out. Here was a plot for a comic opera.

None of this mattered much; the visit became memorable because of the cricket. The MCC team was playing in the only test match of that tour which ended with a result. A large party from the yacht went to the match and and found England with a good lead at the beginning of the West Indies' second innings. Next day we cheered and the yachtsmen threw their caps in the air to celebrate a famous victory, won because Trueman and Statham bowled their hearts out with accurate sustained fast bowling in the blistering heat. I have seen Lindwall and Miller and Lillee and Thompson but those two on that day set a bench mark. They showed the difference between playing flat out for your side and for your country.

That evening we entertained the MCC on board. The two fast bowlers said that they had been much encouraged by the cheers they had heard from the yacht party. Cowdrey was a charming guest and gave me the autographs of the team, greatly increasing the status of my boys at school. I reminded Peter May of a stand we shared together at Chatham in 1948 between the RN Cricket Club and the Eton Ramblers. I was last man and we walked off together at the end of the innings. I had one not out to my name; he was bowled for 202. We put on one run, mine.

The programme included a match between the yacht and the Trinidad police. They batted first and declared. At the tea interval I sat next to a young policeman who was wearing a metal cap on one of his boots. He agreed that he was a quick bowler but not a very successful one.

'Why do you say that?'

'I played for Trinidad against the MCC but I have not yet been picked for a test.'

I was not surprised when he opened the bowling. I said a silent prayer for the leading seaman who always began our innings. Short in stature but big in heart he played an elegant forward defensive shot. As he reached full stretch the ball went over his head from the wicket-keeper on the way back to the bowler.

Cesar (that was his name) shot out the first four before mercy was shown and they took him off to keep the game alive. While their champion was at long-leg or mid-on, two of us, sheltered from the blast, knocked off the runs.

On the last day at Port of Spain, the chief cook was set upon at three in the morning by two thugs and returned with a black eye and swollen face. I sent for him and resisted the urge to sympathise. It was not the first time that I had to bear in mind that this ship was different.

'Do not tell me how, I do not want to know. You are a key senior hand and I depend on you. While you are in this ship you will not go ashore and come off alone in the early hours looking like an ordinary seaman who has lost a fight. That is not an option for a chief petty officer in the royal yacht.'

He looked at me out of his useable eye. We were playing the game to rules that we both understood.

Tobago has had the attention of the package tourists but the white sand and swaying palm trees were still there, together with a rash of new hotels to catch the passing trade. I ate curried land crab in one of them and watched the pelicans swooping after scraps.

At Grenada the almost landlocked harbour of St George is dominated by the 18th century Fort St George at the harbour mouth. A royal salute was fired by a party of locals leaping about amidst the bangs and gunsmoke. Twenty-one guns would have been proper; we gave up counting at thirty-eight and absorbed the beauty of the place. Except for extra buildings and some oil tanks, the soft green hills and white sand, the coloured houses, the English Church by the fort and the fishing boats careening on the beach were there when Rodney's frigates came before the battle of the Saintes in 1782.

We left in the early morning light to call at two more Windward Islands, Carriacou and Bequia, long enough for HRH to visit them. We arrived at Kingston, St Vincent, in the late evening, the last stop in the journey through the Grenadines. Grenada had been a good beginning.

Letter to my wife 10th February, 1960 – St Vincent

I went with Nigel to the administrator's reception; steel band, lovely night and old Georgian government house, now occupied by the West Indian Administrator and his lady. HRH duly walked round the guests and the show was over. Nigel and I then went on to join the wardroom at a grand charity ball. Except that there was a better band and a stone floor it was like a Milstead Cricket Club dance. I asked a six foot six local lady to take the floor and steered her through the throng. The band then started to play 'jump-ups', a kind of local jive, and I lost touch with my partner who began to weave about with a faraway look in her eyes.

The Grenadines are volcanic islands with green hillsides, surrounded by deep blue sea and decorated with solid eighteenth century buildings. St Vincent was the best.

On our first day there my deputy reported that the combination of the main money safe had jammed. I went to the scene and found a collection of well-wishers, mallet wielders and jokers. I reported to the Admiralty what had happened, as required by the regulations. (Their Lordships have a morbid interest in any event involving money) and hired a local locksmith to open it.

He found the main pawl simply worn out and removed the combination, leaving us with £17,000 on a key. The ship was only six years old and the damage could not be put down to fair wear and tear. She must have inherited a safe from another ship.

We played cricket at St Vincent, as expected, and were flattered by the size of the crowd that turned out to see us. We started well and removed their opening batsmen. Number three, Jackson, was ominously good, cutting, pulling and driving anything he thought a poor length ball. He misjudged one in the end and went out to rapturous applause. The crowd then left the ground in silence. It was evident that we had upset them in some way. I hastened to their umpire.

'What is happening?'

'You just bowled Jackson.'

'So what? He was out.'

'These people come to see Jackson bat, not you bowl.'

Thank God it wasn't Sobers.

Barbados is a hundred miles from its nearest comparable neighbour and that may account for the differences we found. The white population is longstanding. We had four days there, while the princess lived ashore. St Lucia came next and, with it, the charm of the islands was back.

Diary 19th February, 1960 – St Lucia

Secured alongside at Port Castries, St Lucia, at 0845, on time. Geoffrey Hawkins on the bridge and I think the admiral showed off a little by coming in too fast. We had to go full astern port and the forefoot touched.
Castries has the bloodiest history of all the West Indian ports – changed hands fourteen times. Old forts and guns everywhere.

Drove up to the Morne Fortune, a collection of fortifications on a hill top in the middle of the island, last used by the British Army in 1903. Memorial to the Enniskillens (27th Foot), who stormed it under Sir John Moore in 1796. They were allowed to fly their King's Colour over the fort for one hour before the Union Flag was hoisted. Cemetery full of soldiers, ensigns and governors, the stuff of empire.
Queen's baby born and we all gathered on the fo'c'stle and gave three cheers for the parents and three more for the baby.

Celebrations for the birth of the new royal prince went on the next day. The chief and petty officers were invited *en bloc* into the wardroom to drink the baby's health in champagne. The yachtsmen were given two tins of beer each for the same purpose, one from the admiral and one from the wardroom. This general relaxation came in the middle of a domestic fracas.

The admiral and the doctor were not getting on and it ended in the latter being sent for officially. He was a strong character with two antarctic expeditions under his belt and a disinclination from time to time to hold his tongue for the good of the service. I pointed out to the admiral that he had never been warned officially and the worst did not occur. The doctor was an asset to the wardroom and we should have missed him.

Dominica is a craggy, noble island whose biggest customer is Rose's Lime Juice. The tin roof of the Dominica Club, where we played tennis, was on a road of shack dwellings with radios blaring 'Crazy Love' and children scampering through the dust.

At lunch time the mainbrace was spliced to mark the final celebration of the birth of Prince Andrew. Coincidentally another classic storm in a tea cup brewed up. The commander told the admiral that cockroaches had come on board with the potatoes at St Lucia. The admiral passed the message on to me, thereby acting as a messenger between his executive and supply officers. I went down with the doctor to look. We found one dead one and no other traces. Nowhere else would priorities and functions be so distorted that three commanders and a vice-admiral became personally involved in the potatoes.

The administrator at Dominica was the Earl of Oxford and Asquith. He came on board with his family, including three girls of five, ten and eleven and a boy of eight. The countess had made herself responsible for the children's education. When they said good-bye the girls curtsied and the small boy bowed to each of us. They were the grandchildren of Raymond Asquith, killed on the Somme at the unusually late age of thirty-five, a classicist of Winchester and Balliol and a paragon of his time.

Montserrat was magnificent from the sea with green volcanic hills beneath the white clouds. We drove through fields of sea island cotton to a beach between two headlands made of black and brown volcanic ash and swarming with land crabs. The heavy swell made swimming difficult and embarrassed some of the guests at HRH's evening reception. The yacht rolled at her anchor while both doctors bustled around with seasick pills. There was only one reported accident, in the stern cabin of our motor boat.

Antigua had enjoyed an important status for many years. The flat coral island was the headquarters of the Leeward Islands station in Nelson's time. The frigates and 74s were warped into English Harbour, now thriving on yachts and the tourist trade. The history will fade but nothing yet has taken away the beauty of the great white painted verandahs of the commodore's house and the 18th century dockyard houses. Nelson sailed to his last battle from here.

After the usual reception we were driven to a barbecue at the Pelican Club where the Brute Force Steel band played and the floor was crowded, among others, with Americans from the missile tracking base and the MCC, here to challenge the Leeward Islands. At the bar Fred Trueman offered me an enormous cigar, one of the many he had been given after the famous victory at

Trinidad. We watched the Leeward Islands bat all day for 220 for five, including 84 from an opener in dirty pads.

On the far side of the ground convicts from the local prison in striped uniforms and hats like Alice's carpenter sat on the grass until called to pull the roller. When the home side did well a little man leapt up and down and did flips on a stick. Anthony Eden arrived and was clapped enthusiastically by the crowd. Cricket mattered, politics did not.

Diary 25th February, 1960 – Antigua

Dinner with a charming farmer and his sister who sold 3000 acres in Kent and bought an island here nine years ago to grow cotton. Then to Government House reception for HRH and a splendid pageant in the garden. Hell's Gate and Brute Force steel bands, choirs, fish dances where the mermaids were chased with determination by fishermen. Slavery ship dances and ghosts, tall and short; the tallest 15 feet high. Backdrop of sugar canes stuck into the ground. Wonderful calypsos – Gunslingers, Sparrow's Cowboy and the favourite, Crazy Love. Man near HRH wore a black Homburg hat the whole evening.

On to St Kitts where we anchored in the bay at Basseterre, where green slopes look down on the houses and the hills of Nevis stand eleven miles to the south. HMS *Troubridge*, the last frigate on the West Indies station, anchored in company. Some of us called on her wardroom and were refreshed to be in a warship again, surrounded by the familiar noises of bosun's pipes, clatter of feet and the hum of auxiliary machinery, where the snow-white teak, wide decks and gold leaf we were used to gave way to semtex, oiled guns and hedgehog mortars.

We won the cricket match, just, because our opening bat closed up one end and we had to play against the clock to get the runs.

Afterwards I asked him why.

'I thought about putting in a few late cuts sir, but decided not.'

The cricket ground had goats on its edges and a mass of small boys surging like starlings from one side of the pavilion to the other. The illegitimacy rate here was one of the highest among the islands.

I met Jim Swanton at an evening party. He thought that some of the governors in the West Indies were now pretending that they were not governors at all. Independence was on the way and attitudes were changing.

At Tortola, in the Virgin Islands, our money was changed into US dollars in deference to the American tourist centre close by at St Thomas. The sailors soon found that they could make a modest killing by putting US 10 cent pieces into the NAAFI drink machine instead of sixpences. In a bid to uphold the law I put a notice in daily orders headed 'Larceny by a Trick'. This did not stop it but brought a petty officer to my cabin with a sheaf of papers about buying his house on mortgage and a request for legal advice.

From the ship it was easy to see the old mule tracks going over the tops of the hills when the slaves had to cultivate everything within reach. I pointed them out to the admiral, who was walking the quarter deck with me.

'Good chaps,' he said.

'Who?'

'Those slaves.'

I was duty commander that day and met HRH at the gangway. She said that she had had a tiring programme and pointed out the white house ashore where she had had lunch. However demanding their schedule had been, the royals usually had a friendly word to the officer who met them.

Bill Pardy reached his 68th birthday on passage from Tortola to Jamaica. The princess invited him to dinner and gave him a wallet. She got it exactly right every time.

Our week in Jamaica was not a roaring success. The shops were geared to the American tourist trade and Mammon ruled.

The navigating officer knew some people at Ocho Rios, on the north coast, and I went with him for a two-day visit to get away from Kingston. We found massive hotels going up there.

Diary 9th March, 1960 – Ocho Rios, Jamaica

Played golf while Peter rode. Dinner at the Marrakech Hotel, still incomplete. Building rubble everywhere but Yanks already in amid the blue and white stucco, Corinthian columns, waiters in black baggy trousers and striped gaiters. The tourists do not look as if they are enjoying it very much but pay the earth for the tasteless food, garish decor and dull company. We were told that they liked to be in the first wave into a new hotel, finished or not. The coast is being ruined by these hideous barracks. Easily the best one was built by a Canadian company in colonial style.

The yacht shifted from Kingston to Port Royal where Fort Charles, built in the 17th century, opened the door to the buccaneer days. We were shown a set of Spanish communion silver given to St Peter's Church by Sir Henry Morgan in a moment of repentance. On the walls were plaque after plaque headed by the names of the ships who had buried their dead here. I remember a frigate with the names of eight lieutenants, midshipmen and warrant officers, most of her officer complement, killed by yellow fever. Nelson had served here. The place brought to mind the price the Royal Navy had paid in the 18th century to keep the merchants rich.

Letter to my wife 13th March, 1960 – Kingston to Belize

One of the nicest of the stewards, Cooper, has had to be flown home with lung trouble. I hope he will be OK; there are a lot of tests to be done that cannot be carried out here. I suppose there is always a possibility that we may take the Armstrong-Jones on their honeymoon. I believe the newspapers are running it.

In Central America the yacht anchored off Belize.

Diary 17th March, 1960 – Belize, British Honduras

Flat and hot. Press conference at the Fort George hotel. 'Conference' of two locals and government house press officer, who did all the talking and needed to change his shirt. Wet and windy trip back; Miss Church, mature member of HRH's staff, nearly broke a bone getting out of the boat.

The cricket team drove through the jungle to the airfield and took on a forward company of the Royal Hampshire Regiment. We changed in their mess and then to dinner with the governor, Sir Colin Thornley, a colonial servant with Uganda experience. Tortoise jelly was followed by tortoise steaks. Tortoises are plentiful in this area. Perhaps they should be protected. The governor's ADC downed a brandy of heroic proportions. At the dance at the Belize Club which followed, the ADC and his wife were the only non-white guests.

One of our engineer lieutenants had an aunt who had come to Belize in 1919 as a member of a nunnery. She had never been home since. All the nuns came on board to see him in a happy, chattering crowd.

The overnight passage from Belize to Grand Cayman was made at 17 knots into a head sea and a 25 knot wind; at midnight the wind freshened and we increased to 19 knots to make our estimated time of arrival. The ship anchored off Georgetown, Grand Cayman next day covered in salt.

One difference between *Britannia* and any other large yacht was her compulsion to arrive on time, whatever the weather. We were not a warship but sometimes ran like one. Our elderly passengers were given a miserable night for no discernable purpose. They made no complaint.

Grand Cayman was well into the American sphere and its connection with London was becoming tenuous. At the usual drink party given by HRH a local came up to me looking anxious.

I asked, 'I see you have a drink. Anything else I can get you?'

'Yes please. I should like an ash tray or a souvenir of some kind.'

'Very sorry but we can't do that.'

'Why not? The Belgian boats always give us something.'

The yacht's final visit in the West Indies was Cockburn Town in the Grand Turk Islands, a two day passage from Grand Cayman. While the ship was at sea the admiral spoke to the yachtsmen and told them that we should be turning round at home and coming back to the West Indies because the Queen had placed the yacht at the disposal of Princess Margaret and Mr Armstrong-Jones for their honeymoon. The news was received cheerfully enough. The ship was on the way back to Portsmouth and they knew that they would soon see their families again.

Grand Turk was another island replete with off-shore companies and beaming bank officials. I was summoned to dine with HRH and sat between Lady Margaret and the wife of the governor of one of the biggest of the other islands. This lady spoke repeatedly about her husband's duties and each time she referred to him as 'HE', indicating her respect for his station. This seemed a good idea. I suggested when back home again that my wife might wish to refer to me in conversation as 'The Commander' instead of 'he' or 'himself' but the offer was declined.

That evening some of us had a long boat ride through the swell in stiff shirts to attend an official cocktail party given on a worn tennis court by the island's administrator. Half the male guests kept their straw hats on and the rest sat on chairs and stared. There were a few American army and navy officers there from their missile tracking station. They seemed bewildered.

On 26th March *Britannia* turned her bows for home. The next day we oiled again from our faithful RFA *Brown Ranger*. They gave us three cheers when they left for Malta. We were sorry to see them go, the band particularly so. They liked enthusiastic audiences and her Maltese seamen always obliged.

In mid-Atlantic the princess decided to do the rounds of the yacht so that everyone had an opportunity of seeing her. She visited the engine room, the galleys and negotiated the iron ladders to the forward messdeck. In the galley the chief cook had laid on frying chips, raw beef, baking bread and the galley staff in perpetual motion. It was a hell's kitchen to look at but the princess was undeterred. She plunged through the maelstrom, asked the right questions and gained an admirer.

'How did it go, chief?'

'Spot on, sir. She was one of the real sort.'

The princess was dined by the wardroom and after dinner I sat next to her while she went through some very old photographs from the *Victoria and Albert*. She seemed to know everyone.

'Ah! That is Paymaster Chapple. He was something in the privy purse after he left the yacht and I used to go to him when I was in trouble – overspent myself and did not want my father to know. He was very helpful.'

I tried to find out who the glamorous Madame de Hautpoul was who appears in many of the Cowes photographs for the twenties but she refused to be drawn.

We arrived off Ponta Delgado in the Azores in a whistling westerly blow with low visibility. The pilot came out in a tiny boat and made it clear that he was boss. We dropped our starboard anchor in the middle of the harbour and turned by wires to buoys, eventually berthing starboard side to. It was complicated and the admiral gave up, repeated the pilots orders and hoped for the best.

On the way home we met heavy weather. The stabilisers were turned off for maintenance without the usual warning and during a bad roll HRH lost the contents of her dressing table. It was an avoidable episode and for once she let it be known that she was not amused.

The yacht went up harbour to South Railway Jetty, Portsmouth, and was met with considerable ceremony. A royal salute was fired and guards and bands paraded at *Dolphin* and *Vernon*. The official party was led by the commander-in-chief Portsmouth and the lord lieutenant of Hampshire, the Duke of Wellington, who both came on board to welcome the princess home. As soon as they had left she inspected the guard on the jetty, waved goodbye from her car and vanished with minimum fuss. The admiral and I were then engaged by the press, who were there in force. They were not interested in our voyage and directed all their questions to the forthcoming honeymoon cruise. Our visit to the West Indies led by the Princess Royal had been welcomed by all she had met, there were no gaffes, no nonsense from the tabloids and much quiet appreciation from all who wished the British well. This was the first year of the sixties; from now on all that was to become old hat.

Halifax to Portsmouth,

8th August, 1959.

H M YACHT BRITANNIA

Memorandum

Wardroom Guest Nights

Without wishing to limit the hour at which Wardroom guest nights or other festivities stop, I consider it important that these should not be overdone. I am sure that 2.45 a.m. is much too late, particularly at sea. There are of course exceptions to every rule.

I would like the senior officers to see that these affairs do not go on extremely late.

VICE ADMIRAL

All Commanders
Surgeon Lieutenant-Commander

Plate 20: 8 August 1959; Remember next time

Plate 21: May 1960; HRH The Princess Margaret's and Mr Armstrong-Jones' honeymoon cruise to the West Indies

98

Chapter 6

HRH THE PRINCESS MARGARET'S HONEYMOON CRUISE 1960

This was my fourth cruise in *Britannia*; it was not particularly long (six weeks) or distant (West Indies) but in retrospect it marked a watershed; the criticism from the media we had noticed in Canada had spread. The UK tabloids carped about her running costs; when she went into Portsmouth Dockyard for maintenance her socialist critics put down parliamentary questions about the cost of each coat of paint on her sides and challenged the expenditure on the pay and allowances of her crew. We were all regulars who had to be paid anyway, wherever we served. Such facts were not allowed to spoil the joy unconfined of knocking the royal family and a fighting service in one blissful strike.

The public approval that *Britannia* enjoyed in her early years thus diminished at a time when it might have been expected to have increased. Her St Lawrence Seaway cruise had demonstrated her value in a way that could hardly have been bettered. It may be that the press developed a resentment at the difficulties they met in getting information about her and those who used her; or perhaps she was just another target in a time of regression, when the workers were told that 'they had never had it so good', the Minister of War lied to Parliament about a whore and the Beatles took the

99

garlands. The public decided it was time to forget 1940 and settle down to a quieter life.

Thirty years later, when the end was approaching, the tabloids smelt a story and decided that they loved her after all and wanted her to be replaced.

She had never been popular to some with influence. The year before I joined her the civil servant head of an important branch at the Admiralty told me that the sooner the Flag Officer Royal Yachts realised that *Britannia* was just another ship in the navy, like the rest, the better it would be. I regarded this as a disloyal and outrageous remark. I see now that it was prescient. Royal yachts like *Victoria and Albert* were built for the sovereign's use in the days when the Royal Navy was an overwhelming weapon built to maintain the nation's seapower. A large royal yacht was a fitting accompaniment to such a force. No more. The navy is small and in ten years the generation will have gone who remember what it feels like to be in a fight *à l'outrance* against a brave and determined enemy. By the time she paid off, the royal yacht shared her function as the personal ship of the sovereign with trade fairs, business conferences and politicians, as in Hong Kong 1997. The connection between her and the warships weakened.

Britannia arrived from the West Indies with the Princess Royal on 7th April 1960 and left to go back there with Princess Margaret twenty-seven days later. This additional cruise took place when the men had been told they would be on leave; they did not learn about the change until the 23rd March. The West Indies were chosen again rather than the Mediterranean.

From the beginning it was apparent that the media could hardly believe their luck. A royal princess was marrying a photographer (albeit one of the Etonian ones) and the hunt for news was on. By today's standards of invasive intrusion their campaign was benign but it displayed a new level of persistence. The yacht was fair game, being part of the wedding scene.

I began to get telephone calls from the press while on leave. When I said nothing, that was news.

The ship's Public Relations Officer, Commander Clarkson, is naturally a harassed man, but he says 'I can't comment; I can only answer questions.' Some questions however he can't answer. They include the furnishings and decorations of the royal suites.

The princess and her husband planned to join the yacht in the Pool of London on the afternoon of their wedding day and leave at once. *Britannia* would carry her off into the western ocean while the world press took the pictures. The Italian paparazzi set the tempo: *Margaret parte verso il suo destino,* drooled *L'Europeo* under a coloured close up of the yacht on its cover page showing the couple on deck as the ship pointed down river. On the wing of the bridge the ship's signal officer, telescope under his arm, looks keenly ahead for flags, while on the deck below a ragged line of unattached yacht officers appear to have wandered out after lunch to see what was afoot. A policeman and a workman on the masonry of Tower Bridge stand to attention while the orderly crowd behind them look respectfully through their binoculars and viewfinders.

The wardroom joined the celebrations the night before when those not on duty were invited by the Queen to attend the wedding ball at Buckingham Palace.

For those with evening dress on board there was only one hurdle to jump before accepting this magnificent invitation, received on the day the ball was held; our wives were all in the country, loaded with children and pleading that they had nothing to wear. Sheila farmed out our six year old and the dogs, bought a new dress, changed in a friend's flat and arrived on the jetty to collect me five minutes late. I thought it better not to ask what had kept her.

We have many memories of that famous night; a cheerful young blonde dressed in yellow silk, wearing a great tiara stuck on her head like a beret, waving an ostrich feather fan to her friends; Earl Attlee, a bent figure in knee breeches looking like a jackdaw; the American ambassador and Mrs Winant hurrying to the floor to support the princess and her future husband who had started the ball alone, and the welcome from Mark Milbank, the Master of the Household, 'Glad you could all make it. This will be the biggest thing since Waterloo.'

Next day colours were at nine o'clock, as usual, and the admiral, commander and officer of the day (all as it happened signal officers by specialisation) attended the ceremony on the fo'c'stle while the band played and the great silk union flag, the biggest the Navy made, was hoisted slowly on the jackstaff before them. Close ahead, the crowds hurrying over Tower Bridge to their offices stopped to watch the ceremony from their perches in the front of the circle.

The yacht seemed quiet that day; the wedding in Westminster Abbey was televised; the hubbub from the traffic and boats died down. As duty commander I was alone in the wardroom while my messmates rooted about London while they could. A messenger called me to the shore telephone.

'Admiral's secretary?'

'Do you know your Jack is upside down?'

'Who is speaking?'

'I am an ex-lieutenant-commander RNVR. I have just walked across the bridge and seen it. Go and look.'

'I will. Thank you.'

He was right of course. Worse, the press got hold of it. The signal lieutenant, as officer of the day, was given a hard time by the admiral, who was horrified. He saw it as a public humiliation although the explanation was simple. The dockyard had sewn the toggle (a small pin of wood put through the eye of a rope) at the wrong end of the flag, no one spotted it, and it went up the wrong way before three signal officers, the Royal Marine band and a crowd of city workers. Any Boy Scout would have known that the royal yacht had hoisted a signal of distress. The comedy was not over.

At lunch time the officer of the watch asked me to come to the gangway where I found a thin young man in glasses with an earnest expression and a brown envelope.

'I have an urgent message from a goverment department for the admiral.'

'I will take it.'

'My orders are that I hand it to the admiral personally.'

'He is having lunch with his wife. Give it to me and I will see what I can do.'

Half way up the ladder I did what I should have done at once and opened the letter:

To the Flag Officer, Royal Yachts.
The Editor and readers of the Daily Sketch *wish you a happy and safe voyage.*
Editor

I bounded down and found him skulking in a corner of the upper deck taking photographs at the rate of knots. I took his camera and ordered the quartermaster to keep him on the gangway. The boatswain, who was officer of the watch, told me later that he was ready to grab me because he thought that I would throw him over the side. This was never in my mind but I do remember calling him an impudent clown who ought to be made to swim ashore. We sent him away; adverse publicity on the happy day was to be avoided. His editor undertook not to publish the photographs. Nowadays, when his camera could have been a grenade, he might have ended up assisting MI6 with their enquiries.

The royal party was on board by 1730. On the way down river the noise from helicopters, crowds and ship sirens challenged the music from the 30-strong Royal Marine band. The princess, in a yellow suit with a yellow turban hat, stayed on the royal bridge while daylight lasted so that the crowds could see her. The band left us off Southend, together with a stoker on compassionate leave, whose father was dying, and the yacht headed for the Channel.

Forty-eight hours later we were a hundred miles SSW of Ushant and thumping into a moderate sea. The admiral and the one equerry in the royal party were alone in the royal dining room, while the yacht sailed on westwards like the *Marie Celeste*, her destination undecided.

Diary 9th May, 1960 – London to West Indies

Dined aft with Admiral, Griffin (equerry) and North. Dull evening. I had not realised the national significance of the fall in attendance at the Eton-Harrow match.

10th May

Off St Miguel, Azores. Island covered in black rain clouds. Sea dark, confused, menacing.

12th May

Blue sea and sky. Into tropical rig. A young cook cheeked a petty officer cook in the galley and will have to be dismissed the yacht service. It was only a slip of the tongue but bloody-mindedness is serious.

Decision at last. Admiral told to take her to Tobago and Trinidad to begin with.

We were dogged by trivia: the mail was sent to Grenada, not Trinidad, because the obsession with privacy delayed our programme signal to the Admiralty; the new rubber swimming bath collapsed and is beyond repair; a signalman barged on to the veranda deck to hoist a flag and the admiral heard about it from the princess; a steward, thinking it empty, entered the royal suite; the Governor General at Trinidad wants photographs to keep the local press quiet; the UK press made a moronic signal addressed to 'The Master, HM Yacht *Britannia*', asking for our position and estimated time of arrival. It was signed 'Watkins and Hopkins, *Daily Mirror* and *Daily Express*'.

The yacht anchored off Tobago on the 17th May and was met by an aeroplane full of paparazzi and a radio commentator. Any further attempt at secrecy was pointless. Two days later we were at Port of Spain, Trinidad, where the princess was met by the governor-general, governor, prime minister and a steel band before driving to Government House. As the royal barge came alongside to bring her back the gangway lights went out, too late to stop the barge. This was the first time it had happened, and probably the last.

That night there was a fracas ashore in a night club and four of our stokers were hurt; one nearly lost his ear. The next day we left for the Tobago Cays in the Grenadines, a small circular chain of reefs south of Bequi. Here privacy could be guaranteed. The yacht anchored off Petit Rameau, recommmended to us by the governor.

The coxswain of the motor boat reported that the place looked superb but the beach was taken by three scruffy Frenchmen. I went in with the sub-lieutenant and found two men in hammocks while a third, the cook, prepared a meal over a driftwood fire. Empty bottles lay about and the general mess suggested that they had been there for some days. They told me that they had come from Martinique on a fishing trip. I said that we had come from the UK on a honeymoon trip and if they would care to go to the point they would see my ship waiting with two hundred men for them to go away so that HM the Queen's sister and her husband could land on this scrap of the British Empire for a picnic. At least that was what I meant to say; my French varied but they got the drift.

'Il n'est pas possible.'

'Pourquoi?'

'Nous n'avons pas assez d'essence pour le bateau.''

'Nous le vous donnerons.'

'OK.'

Our petrol stocks were limited, being used only for the ship's boats, but we found enough to get rid of them. A party of sailors cleaned up the mess and paradise was regained. It was a place of intense blue water and white sand; the bellies of the swooping noddys and terns reflected the blue of the sea.

The yacht shifted twenty miles to Mustique, for two hundred years the site of two prosperous sugar plantations before it was abandoned. Manchineel bushes proliferated, with their poisonous latex sap. The Tennants bought it for a song and were clearing it up before selling off plots to their friends.

Dominica, with its volcanic sand and underdeveloped economy came next. HRH drove across the island and the yacht picked her up on the other side before making the short trip to St John's Antigua and a day of confusion.

The plan was to disembark the royals at St John's and give the yachtsmen leave there. The ship would then go to English Harbour to collect HRH before returning to St John's for the sailors. At English Harbour we burned two large signal lamps on the cliffs to help the barge's crew while the yacht lay off. We left two hours late, when HRH got back, and our libertymen were not on board until after midnight. The admiral learned for the first time that evening that the yacht would be required to stay in Antigua for an extra six days before sailing for home.

The island offered excellent beaches for picnics and bathing and the yachtsmen were encouraged to make the most of them. The response was subdued, which was unusual. I believe it may have been because, for the first time, *Britannia* was being used like other yachts – for pleasure, with the owner on board and deciding where to go next. This was a new routine.

The wardroom organised a beach picnic opposite the ship. We

had the Hell's Gate steel band, a large fire and a barbecue. The ship was illuminated, a mile away, and the moon shone. The setting was as perfect as these things can be. The royal passengers were our guests. In due course one or two of our messmates were tossed into the sea. There was nothing untoward about that on such occasions. Major Griffin, who was popular among us, was next and found it funny. The barge was summoned at once and our distinguished guests left, taking their soaking equerry with them. Each one of us felt that he had two left feet.

Diary 7th June, 1960 – Antigua

The driver of my taxi had a photograph in his cab.
'Who's that?'
'That's my wife. She has been in England for three years now.'
'Why aren't you there?'
'I do not know. Sheer negligence I suppose.'

The chief cook came to see me. He wants to go back to general service. He has only one year to do. I sorted out his moans. I hope he will forget it.

On the way home the royal couple went the rounds in the ship and gave the yachtsmen the first opportunity most of them had had to see them. In the ship's company galley the chief cook explained the beauties of ox hearts to the princess, who seemed bewildered. The chief tried a practical demonstration and beat his breast,
    'You know, ma'am, in 'ere – cows' 'earts.'
    'I follow. But I think all innards are awful, don't you?'

There was a heavy fog in the Needles Channel. We went southabout past the Nab Tower and were alongside at Portsmouth on 18th June 1960, Waterloo Day. From time to time the cruise had seemed a close run thing too.

Plate 22: March 1960: HRH The Princess Royal's tour of the West Indies

Chapter 7

COWES AND HOME WATERS 1960

The Victorian royal yachts went to Cowes every year and *Britannia* continued the tradition. Cowes, like Ascot, Goodwood, Lords for the Eton-Harrow match, and Henley became part of the season's ritual for the Edwardian upper classes. It had close connections with royalty: Queen Victoria made a home at nearby Osborne, King Edward VII and King George V enjoyed racing in the big yachts and the Royal Yacht Squadron was there.

This yacht club obtained royal permission for its members to wear the white ensign.

For many years, up to the Second World War, the annual cruise from Portsmouth to Cowes was the only sea time *Victoria and Albert III* served. She raised steam, shut down her boilers and completed the eight mile journey on that head of steam without a speck of soot coming out of her funnels to soil the teak on her upper deck.

1960 was a bumper year. As well as *Britannia*, HMS *Dainty*, a guided missile destroyer, acted as guardship, together with a minesweeper from the London Division RNR and a tank landing ship. Foreign navies were represented by the American destroyer USS *Barry* and the French FS *Pollux*. *Barry* distinguished herself by using a white nylon anchor cable; *Pollux* by arriving late and anchoring in the wrong place.

Diary 30th July, 1960 – Cowes

Wardroom invited to an Osborne House garden party. Victoriana Majestica. Christ descending from the cross in Queen Victoria's bedroom, bronze plaque over the bed, sachet for Prince Albert's watch and a brutal display af deer heads in the Horn Room. Examined a photograph album in the Durbar Room of the Khartoum Expedition. It was devoted to the blood and guts of infantry warfare. Page after page of the Seaforths burying their dead. Glass cases of plaster casts of the children's arms and legs on velvet cushions. Here was sewing, gossip, family love and Germanic taste at the zenith of the Empire. Not recognisable as an Englishman's castle.

The admiral, accompanied by his secretary and flag lieutenant, called on the Royal Yacht Squadron. We landed at the squadron steps and were received by the secretary, a retired RN captain employed by the club. One or two members among the box hedges and Victorian stonework raised their yachting caps in tentative greeting. We had sherry with the secretary and then to church where the admiral and the captain of *Dainty* read the lessons.

An old steam yacht with delightful lines, wearing the squadron white ensign, anchored near to us. She had been chartered for the week by a party of plump young men who spent much of the time on her upper deck, glasses in hand, watching the racing. We received a handwritten note from her asking for our boats to slow down when they ran past because they found the wash irritating.

The yacht left on the fifth day for Cardiff where the Queen embarked for her visit to Shetland and Orkney. Charles, Anne and the young Kents arrived the next day and we headed north, with *Duncan*, a small frigate commanded by a bewhiskered aviator, in line astern. She came dangerously close on two occasions; the first time we went full ahead to get clear of her.

That evening the Queen entertained the wardroom to drinks and we were all presented, old and new. The atmosphere was relaxed. The children ran all over the ship playing games and making apt remarks. Charles ran into me:

'You have got nothing to do I suppose?'

Compared with a job in the fleet, I had not. That was the snag and he guessed it.

The Isle of Man was passed at 18 knots and we scampered through the Western Isles in bright sunlight, anchoring off Weavers Point in the Sound of Harris at nearly midnight. Pilot found a rock giving 6 fathoms instead of the 12 fathoms shown on the chart. He spent the rest of the night in a boat with a lead line until he was satisfied that the rock was isolated.

Four of us walked the heather, peat and ponds of North Uist; to the north lay Harris, south, South Uist and south-east, Skye. We lay in the heather on top of a hill and looked at St Kilda, forty miles out in the Atlantic. In the years to come it would always be bright morning there.

Next day we left for Lerwick; while we were at sea I was summoned to dine with the Queen. I sat on her right with Prince Charles on my right. She liked lobsters. The Hebrides seemed so romantic but the sea is always romantic. Her brother-in-law had a studio at Rotherhithe and says that the Thames always looks different. The tide may cause that, ma'am, but artists always see things differently. Did you see St Kilda today, ma'am? Yes. I should not have thought it possible at forty miles. The cliffs are 1000 feet high, ma'am. Yes, I am afraid my mathematics are not good. There seem to be a lot of Russian trawlers about. We were told at the staff college, ma'am, that 1000 Russian ships are in the North Atlantic at any one time. Then about Gary Powers and nuclear sufficiency and the Common Market.

I am told that the Old Commonwealth want us in the Common Market, ma'am. Ah! but what about the business people in Australia, they would lose money and not like it. I suppose it depends upon whether politics come before economics, ma'am. Marx thought they did. Man cannot live by bread alone.

The conversation was then changed effortlessly away from the political bog into which I had floundered. Yes, I have seen the Flannen Isles, ma'am. I was a cadet then, coming back from Iceland. It was our first landfall in the gale and immensely cheering. Had I been to Iceland and what was it like? Interesting, ma'am, but that was before the war. I had not seen it since the occupation. Occupation? Did I mean the Americans? Laughter. Perhaps I should have said investment. The Chief of the Defence Staff said how like the Americans to tell Powers that his aircraft would explode if he tried to eject.

Dinner was then half finished and conversation was directed for the rest of the meal to the second lieutenant, the guest sitting on the Queen's left. My turn was over.

The concert party performed in the dining room, which was soon made ready. Charles and Anne took part as assistants, a wardroom choir sang in mess undress, the first lieutenant played 'The Saints Came Marching In' on a borrowed trombone and the sailmaker reduced the audience to incoherence. He asked for the hardest worked man in the yacht to stand. The admiral stood up and was told to sit down. He then became a parson before putting on an old fashioned ladies' hat and mimicking – God, will he get away with it? – the Princess Royal.

After the show the party went to the anteroom in good humour. The Queen sent seventeen-year old Prince Michael to bed and announced that he was still recovering from the long train journey to Loch Ewe with the Eton OTC. The train was late and the boys were not fed. Princess Alexandra played the piano in the drawing room and I thought that this was the life I liked but not the one I got.

The pretty flags over the granite houses at Lerwick were stiff in the northerly wind. The Queen went ashore to carry out her engagements and the yacht left with *Duncan* to breast a northerly gale, on passage for Toft's Voe on the other side of Shetland, where she would re-embark later in the day. On arrival we drifted about in an eight knot tide race trying to anchor. She held in the end but the admiral stayed on the bridge until we could leave.

A helicopter from the Queen's Flight with the mail found a flat space to land north of the village and we sent a boat through the weather to get it. Because of the conditions the commander went in with the royal barge and I took his place to meet the Queen when she returned. She let out an expressive sigh when she stepped on board. The children arrived in the wardroom and announced with pride that they had felt sick in the boat. We sailed at once and anchored in more comfortable conditions two hours later at Fetlar, leaving the doctor, signal officer and one of the lady clerks ashore to be brought on by *Duncan*.

Diary 11th August, 1960 – Fetlar to Scapa

Left Fetlar at 0800 and arrived Balta Sound at 0935. Gale from north. A bewildering day when we went from island to island to land the Queen for short visits in bright sunshine and cool wind. Uyea Sound, Mid Yell, Out Skerries and Whalsay came and went. Whalsay looked attractive, with a southerly cove and a big shuttered Georgian house on the hill. Small sailing boats, well-handled by a man and a boy, raced about the anchorage.
We arrived at Fair Isle when the light had almost gone. Some debate on the bridge about where to anchor and whether or not to follow a small boat trying to show us the way. Eventually we let go in 26 fathoms and HM and HRH went in for a one hour visit. It was almost dark then. The locals lit a bonfire. We left without Duncan, *messing about in the heavy swell trying to recover her boat, filled with pressmen who must have been tempted to express views about the arrangements.* Duncan *then detached ahead to make good defect in her main feed regulator at Scapa.*

Britannia went through the Flow to Stromness where the Queen disembarked for her Orkney tour while we went westabout to Kirkwall to wait for her.

The old hands looked again at Flotta and Longhope. *Britannia* would not have existed if the Grand Fleet in the First War and the Home Fleet in the Second had not done the business from here. Royal yachts are the icing on the cake of sea power.

After short visits to Stronsay and Westray the Queen's Orkney and Shetland tour was over. She disembarked at Aberdeen after greeting Prince Andrew (six months) who was brought on board for breakfast. The yachtsmen had a motor cutter with a fouled screw and broken motor boat davits to repair. The Queen had completed a relentless three-day programme, much of it by boat in a seaway, and some clearing up was expected.

On the way south, the wardroom dined the leavers and Bill Pardey to celebrate Bill's fifty years service, nearly all of it at sea. From Jellicoe to Mountbatten – Bill saw it all.

Chapter 8

STATE VISITS TO TUNISIA AND ITALY – 1961

THE SIX MONTHS IN DOCKYARD HANDS in the 1960-61 winter ended with sea trials. Two problems defied the technical experts then. First, the habit of the mizzen mast of vibrating at the yacht's economical speed of twelve knots. The mizzen was there for show, to find room for an extra masthead flag and to make her look pretty when dressed overall. On the down side it stopped helicopters landing. The mast went through the royal sleeping apartments, a box on the after end of the upper deck. When the mizzen was vibrating the noise resonated inside the box.

The lining in the royal drawing room was stripped out in the hope of packing the mast into silence. It did not work although the opportunity was used to remove some workmen's sandwiches, left behind the panelling eight years before when she was completing at John Brown's.

The second problem was also attributable to a defect in design. Her boilers burned furnace fuel oil, a heavy oil used by much of the navy at one time. The fleet changed to diesel and *Britannia* found it increasingly difficult to refuel unless she had her own oiler with her. Trials were carried out to persuade the boilers to burn diesel but success had not been achieved at that time.

On Friday, 14th April, 1961 the yacht waited alongside South Railway Jetty. A royal guard from HMS *Excellent,* the gunnery school, were fallen in by the gangway while HMS *Forth,* a submarine depot ship berthed astern, manned ship. A royal motorcade swept on to the jetty, the guard presented arms, *Forth* began a deafening gun salute and HM Queen Elizabeth, the Queen Mother, embarked in *Britannia* for her official visit to Tunisia. We left with our silk flags cracking in the wind and the frigate *Salisbury,* our ocean escort, following behind. HM the Queen Mother would visit Tunisia and disembark in Sardinia, where HM the Queen would embark for her state visit to Italy. The Duke of Gloucester, as president of the War Graves Commission, would then use the yacht to visit war graves in the Mediterranean.

On the way south we rounded Ushant at lunch time on the second day and the household called on the wardroom. Bernard Fergusson, a soldier turned author and a known raconteur, was in the party. He told me that his father had commanded a division in France in the Great War. The division had no radio and one motor car (his father's private property).

Queen Elizabeth, the Queen Mother, called on the wardroom that evening with Lady Fermoy and Mrs Mulholland, who were attending her. We were all presented and HM talked to everybody. She seemed interested in everything that was said to her. The ship was rolling and she leant against a bulkhead for support while Captain McLean, RM, the Director of Music, and I gathered round. 'Bandy', as McLean was known, began a summary of the discords in the Tunisian national anthem. HM caught my eye and we both began laughing.

'I thought you looked a little bewildered.'
'Above my head, I am afraid, ma'am.'

I showed her some of the things we had in the mess and she took great interest in a glass case with a piece of coral given to us by Princess Margaret. She gave her complete attention to whoever she was listening to.

The wind freshened during the night and it was blowing hard next morning. Off Cape Rocca the P&O liner *Himalaya*, carrying the Australian cricket team, passed on the opposite course close down our starboard side. The passengers, largely Australian, massed to see us and waved and cheered as we went by. Queen Elizabeth stood alone on the heaving royal deck, where they could see her best, and waved back. Everyone who saw it felt rather full.

I was summoned to dine and sat on Queen Elizabeth's right, with Mrs Mulholland on the other side. I remember how much I enjoyed it and would willingly, had she asked me if I agreed with her, have concurred that the Commonwealth came before the Common Market, big ships were needed in the Royal Navy, cruisers should be commissioned for training, Russians were communists because they were childish and leaders in politics were a bad thing. I was able to reassure her that she would find it easy to get ashore at Tunis in the evenings 'in tiaras and things' because we went down a long canal to get there and could berth in comfort.

As it turned out I was wrong about that. The best came last.

'I see you were in the war. How old were you when it started ?'

'Eighteen, ma'am.'

'Aha! Just right!'

Given an hour with Hitler she would have charmed him like she did everybody else and there might have been no war.

We arrived alongside at Gibraltar twenty seconds late and left that evening with the admiral's old ship, the Battle class destroyer *Saintes*, as escort. She no longer had the black top to her funnel she had as leader of the Third Destroyer Squadron when he commanded her.

The French destroyer *Le Bourdonnais* came out from Oran and escorted us for a half an hour, firing a royal salute and manning ship. She cruised silently past, her sailors immobile and well turned out. It was dignified and impressive, more so perhaps because they must have known that we were going to Tunis where

117

the Algerians were popular. The news came through that there had been a military coup in Algiers that day. The admiral received a signal from the commander-in-chief Mediterranean saying that *Saintes* might have to leave us at no notice.

Diary 24th April, 1961 – Tunis

Still blowing hard from NW and Saintes *yawing about all over the place. News from Algeria bad. The French have it all (i.e. army in revolt). Admiral worried about attempting the canal passage from La Goulette to Tunis in the force 8 wind. The canal is 150 feet wide and six miles long. Embassy unhelpful. Decided to anchor off and send HM up in the barge. The weather very wet for the barge. When ambassador arrived in pilot boat it was decided to attempt the passage in the yacht. Ambassador in cocked hat, very composed.*
With him Maltese vice-consul, not composed. We gave him six whiskies in Hallam's cabin and he seemed better. The yacht went up the canal crab-wise, the wind very strong. Our tattered royal standard replaced just before berthing. This was immediately reduced to tatters as well. A catamaran which looked like a football pitch being moved from our berth as we came in. President's Spahis on the jetty. Enormous Arabs with drawn sabres and childlike bewildered expressions. HM inspected the guard while the band played one thin, flat tune, and then disappeared into the shed, a vision in blue among the sea of black coats and faces. The Rolls Royce was disembarked with every seaman officer taking charge, including the admiral, while the boatswain brushed aside a very Europeanised Arab insisting in a hysterical voice that these sorts of jobs in the harbour were his alone.

25th April, 1961 – Tunis

Wind now dropped. During the forenoon the captain of Saintes

118

brought over a warrant for 60 days detention for the Admiral to approve. Our mail has gone to pot because de Gaulle has stopped all night flights to Paris. Norman Blacklock and I were swindled in a carpet shop and got out with difficulty. They are as keen as ever to gather tourist money but no longer willing to oblige.

Met the guests for HM's dinner for the president. Succession of neatly dinner-jacketed small-footed dark men in dark glasses with rounded young women. The president's bodyguard followed him into the dining room and were extracted by the admiral with difficulty. A press man got up one gangway and was sent whistling down another. Three guests did not turn up and the president's aide came out to use the telephone to find them. M. Abasi and wife not coming because his mother was ill. Third guest has vanished. A bodyguard asked me whether I was married and how many women I was allowed. The president had just decreed that they could only have one each.

After it was over HM kept the ambassador talking inside while Fergusson and the first secretary brayed away on the upper deck in full voice exchanging identifications and dropping names to the stupefaction of those on duty who had to listen. The embassy has no grounds for satisfaction. They cannot find a car for the admiral and there is zero entertainment for the officers or yachtsmen.

Queen Elizabeth attended a gala gorgeously dressed in white and diamonds and listened to Arab music for two and a half hours. The theatre manager, seemingly terrified, lowered the curtain when the choir were in the middle of their piece. We heard them, undeterred, as they carried on behind the barrier. A Bedouin belly dancer stole the show. She remained well covered for her act, in deference to the royal guest, but managed to persuade her abdomen to oscillate at a remarkable rate for a remarkable time, to the astonishment and admiration of the audience.

The yacht went independently to Sousse the next day and waited for Queen Elizabeth. President Bourguiba came to say goodbye although protocol required his presence for a head of state only. It was a heavy send off, backed by a hundred-strong band, a royal guard in blue uniforms, a line of politicians and diplomats, a corps of young girls from the Jeunesse Bourguiba in red tracksuits and the usual Spahis.

The harbour was awkward and we left stern-first and recovered our boats outside. A battery of field guns on the beach fired a royal salute and shook everything that moved on board.

Next day the commander-in-chief, Mediterranean, joined in his yacht *Surprise* and slipped into place between us and *Saintes* with professional ease. She was commanded by David Scott, an old friend from gunroom days in *Revenge*. Off Cagliari the escorts stayed outside the harbour until the yacht had secured bow and stern to the two buoys waiting for us.

We lowered two boats, one to take the bow lines and one for the stern. What happened next was never publicly discussed. There was no enquiry and we forgot about it. That tended to be a yacht speciality when things went wrong. I can only report what I saw and heard.

The ship had to manoeuvre to get the bow line on first. The wind may have blown her down, or the wash from the screws caught the boat with the stern line, but for whatever reason the boat ahead was held up and could make no progress towards her buoy. This was reported to the admiral who ordered the picking up rope aft to be slipped. The rope went over the side, followed by the wire, still attached to it. Great bights of rope and wire finished up in Cagliari harbour. The starboard screw wrapped the picking up rope round it. This rope is designed to float but was taken down by the weight of several tons of the attached wire. The engine room reported that the port propeller shaft had jammed. Two Queens of England wanted to use the ship that day. She was secured but immobile.

The engineer officer appeared on the bridge; an unusual

occurrence when the ship was manoeuvring. No one risked saying anything.

'Do I understand, chief,' said the admiral in a flat, rather bored voice as he faced the probability that he would have to tell the Queen, on her way by air, that the yacht she required for her state visit could not move, 'that I am without any engines at all?'

'The engines cannot be used until the screws are cleared sir.'

Our divers went down. The starboard screw was soon cleared of rope. The port shaft had twenty-six turns of wire round it which would have to be cut off. This needed special equipment which we did not have. The Sardinian liaison officer produced an Italian diving party but they made no progress. The commander-in-chief in *Surprise* got us out of it. The Fleet Clearance Diving Team happened to be on passage from Malta to Spezia in a tug. They were diverted by the C-in-C by signal from *Surprise* and arrived later that day. An underwater cutting set was flown to Cagliari from Malta in a Scimitar jet fighter and arrived at 0700 next day. The RN diving team slogged away at the wire and cut it off nineteen hours later.

Meanwhile the Queen arrived on board in pouring rain to be told that there might be a delay. The Queen Mother left shortly afterwards. The immediate problem changed from the screw to making a suitable alternative programme for the Queen during the waiting time. All hands gathered round the pump.

Diary Saturday 29th April, 1961 – Cagliari

During the dog watches the Sardinian liaison officer and I stayed on the telephone trying to get hold of Lombard-Hobson, the naval attaché, who had come on board and then disappeared. We sent an officer ashore and found him at last. After dinner Adeane, the Queen's secretary, called a meeting in the admiral's cabin to discuss an alternative programme for to-morrow if the repairs were delayed. Colville, press secretary, Charteris, assistant secretary and Lombard-Hobson made up the party. The household in a relaxed mood. The schadenfreude of having one of their number i.e. the admiral, on the rack may have helped. Adeane smoked a cigar between one finger and thumb and sometimes fell from his position of eminence grise *and giggled; Charteris sensible; Colville trying to spot the winner; Admiral carefully choosing his words. Reuters rang later and I gave them the story. Admiralty had not got our earlier signal and understood from Reuters that the yacht had been in an accident. Ended the day by shaking Colville during the middle watch and telling him about Reuters.*

We left next morning for Naples and the state visit. The household in attendance filled the wardroom when they came for drinks. Earl Alexander was wearing an XL tie and I talked cricket with him. He was a short man with no affectations of any kind, straight and true.

The admiral took prayers on the forecastle. Afterwards he explained to the yachtsmen how the screw had been fouled and thanked them for their efforts in getting the ship ready for the important visit ahead.

We anchored off the Lipari Islands, north of Sicily, while the Queen lunched ashore. Three fishing boats spotted us and the *Daily Express* reported next day what the Queen had eaten for lunch. While this was going on *Saintes* was detached and hid herself round the nearest headland to paint her bow where her anchor had scored it. At 2200 the cruiser, *Lion*, and another big destroyer, *Solebay*, joined the escort. Our military splendour was complete.

Diary Monday 1st May, 1961 – Cagliari to Naples

About to turn in at 2330 when Charteris arrived in my cabin. The bandsmen are being flown home from Naples and one of

them has passed a message through a footman to him asking
for a car from Buckingham Palace to take four of them from
London Airport to London. Told him to leave it to me. He
chatted for a while and left.

Early on the big day the Italian escort appeared through haze and
sunshine. A destroyer leader, *San Giorgio* led, followed by two
frigates. They took station on our starboard quarter with *Lion*,
Saintes and *Solebay* on the opposite side. Capri appeared ahead
and it looked as if *Lion* and company might be scraped off until
both squadrons formed line astern behind *Britannia* as we passed
close by the island. An old Roman ruin crowned the highest cliff.
David said that the Emperor Tiberius held his orgies there and
threw the remains, including the women and boys, over the cliff. I
asked whether his memory was equally good on the Latin irregular
verbs.

Diary 2nd May, 1961 – Naples

The squadron cleared the Capri channel at 0845 and the
Italians passed close by in turn. They cheered in an odd way,
raising their hands above their heads quickly and bringing
them down to their sides. Each cheer is controlled from the
bridge and there is a measurable time between them. It was
more ordered than our system which attempts a controlled
spontaneity and needs much rehearsal to look good. The
Italians were well handled and smart. The officers were in a
line with their blue sashes and looked impressive. The British
ships passed too far away. We entered Naples with San
Giorgio *alone, gun salutes about us and the harbour alert with*
expectation. I took charge of the piping on the port side,
remembering hard not to salute as Her Majesty was on deck. A
USN depot ship with a clutch of destroyers were all manned as
we passed them. I sounded the 'carry on' too soon and we

passed the last trot of destroyers with their hands stood at ease. No one noticed in the excitement. Piping was going on furiously from our other side and the ceremonial became scrambled. The sight of two beautiful ships coming into a famous harbour attracted all the attention. The admiral brought her in quickly and perfectly, five seconds too early, and aroused the interest of Prince Philip.

'The wind helped you.'

Jetty filled with the usual dignitaries, the red carpet laid into the middle distance, palm fronds, little girls with flowers, a horde of TV people on top of a concrete shelter, including Dimbleby, who had talked to me at Portsmouth about this moment.

San Giorgio *came in smartly and secured stern to the wall behind us. The orders required* Lion *to do the same ahead of us but she decided against it and came in after the spectators had gone.*

The Queen landed followed by her household army, inspected a moderate naval guard and marched up the carpet with the marvellous idle walk she has. The cortège left the jetty, the band marched off, the Italian guard commander bounced up and down to the music on the balls of his feet; Britannia's *royal duty was over for the time being.*

Pompeii – The guide had a jokey sort of English and used it without mercy. 'The Romans were up to date: see-wine cooler made deep freeze; these granite chips like cats eyes in the road! The straight granite flagstones and distant columns made a clear and compelling picture. A calcified dog with a collar stood where the ashes and gas from Vesuvius had choked him in AD 79. The pictures on the red stucco walls had cream cheese in them to preserve the colour. Lead from Cornwall tin mines made the damp courses and internal drainage pipes. Sex, of course, was known to the Romans and their uninhibited treatment of it has kept the tourists coming. The face of the boy and the tiger shows lust as well as fear and triumph. The oil lamps have three or four spouts of penal shape. A bronze statue was dull and green with age except for the genitalia, bright from the hands of the curious through the centuries. Outside the hawkers sell small silver tricked phalluses, anxious to satisfy the market. A carrotzi horse munched oats and dreamt visibly of love. What do they do on their days off?

We went through the Straits of Messina and up the Adriatic to Ancona.

Diary 5th May, 1961 – Naples to Ancona

Monte Canero abeam at 0845. I came near it in a Dakota in a snowstorm in 1944. Ancona harbour still a shambles. Italian royal yacht still on her beam ends. Jetties with the same bomb holes that were there in the summer of 1944. Ran into Bill Burns, the assistant naval attaché at Rome. We know each other but neither can remember where. He produced a car and we went up to Osimo. I knew the family were all in Rome. The Piazza Dante scruffy. Piero's world was vanishing. The house needed paint and repair. It was a beautiful day, warm sun and the smell of hay from the fields. The lanes made clean white scars over the olive groves. We looked across at Offagna and Monte Canero and drove past Francesca's villa with the great earthenware pots and green trees. The workers' flats are going up now and the big houses have office signs outside them; the hammer and sickle hang over the party office in the main square and grass is growing on the roofs.

The Duke and Duchess of Gloucester embarked with Lady Angela Dawnay, a sister of the duchess, as a lady in waiting. The

125

Queen came later and the yachtsmen got ready for sea. Someone said that the press secretary had gone ashore to telephone and had not returned. The order came to leave nevertheless. The brow to the shore was removed and the lines taken off. The yacht was moving slowly across the basin when the press secretary appeared, running along the jetty like a stag, to the delight of those on our upper deck and the cheers of the locals ashore. We stopped and lowered a boat for him. The press secretary, frantic because he had kept the sovereign waiting, went too fast and got hung up on some wire guardrails before making a three point landing with arms and legs in the bottom of the boat. He put everyone into a good humour.

One day in Venice was spent with two anchors down, secured by the stern off the Piazza San Marco. *Solebay* did the same and the tourists had a good view. St Mark's Cathedral was there, darkly Byzantine with gloomy curving arches and the dull glitter of old gold. The floor is gently undulating, like a field. The supports are wooden stakes driven into the earth 1500 years ago and swollen together like cement. The water has probably got into them by now and, together with the weight of marble and bronze, has made them weary. St.Mark's Square was stiff with tourists, staring with dull expressions and talking in indiscernible tongues. When I first saw this place it was dotted with New Zealand soldiers and laughing young women. I ate a solitary dinner on board and watched a firework display which filled the harbour with smoke, reducing the fireworks to a dull glow.

Next day the Queen disembarked to return home and *Britannia* set out for Athens with the Duke of Gloucester who was booked to open a memorial to the last war dead. He visited the wardroom, a stooped figure. It must be a lottery whether he can complete the arduous tour of the war graves that has been set for him.

In Athens I was hit for six and went over the top.

Diary 10th May, 1961 – Athens

Tilley and I went in the jeep to the Acropolis. The Parthenon is the most beautiful thing I have ever seen. Its strength is vast, with huge Doric columns, yet it is built with the precision of a watch. The marble steps fall by six inches to remove the rain. On hands and knees, looking along it, the curve seemed perfect. It is timeless, a glorious relic of civilised man and stands between heaven and earth on the top of that ancient hill with the inevitability of something made in perfect proportion in the best setting. As we went up, the view got better, the walk more absorbing. The final sight of the Parthenon is like the climax of a great work of music. In its complete state it must have been unendurably beautiful and in its ruins it has soared above death and destruction. Shattered and broken, it lifts its head between earth and sky, indestructible, the essence of the spirit of man. I have never seen anything like it and shall never forget it.

A heavy swell stopped our boats running at Athens. The yacht shifted berth to go alongside at Piraeus to enable the dinner party for the King and Queen of Greece to take place.

Next day at sea the captain of *Saintes* was transferred by high wire to lunch with the admiral. He brought seven punishment warrants for detention with him for the admiral to approve. His sailors had got into a row in a cafe and gathered over a hundred furious Greeks round them. *Saintes* wanted the sentences suspended but the admiral said they must be served. Visits by HM ships had only recently re-started to Greece. He wants the sailors to be discouraged from too much oozou and happy punch-ups ashore there.

I was summoned to dinner with Prince Henry and sat next to him. He spoke at length about Kenya, I believe. I cannot be certain because I found his voice hard to hear. He had a favourite story about taking a ciné film of wildlife and then finding that the cover

127

was on the lens.

At Salonika a storm came from the hills and washed down the dirt roads, white shacks and flower beds of green painted oil drums. The sea front, a desert of wet stone with no rails where it met the sea, was empty. A British and French army was sent here in 1917. The graves were ornate and scattered. I looked back through the downpour on the way to the ship; British sea-power had enabled the soldiers to fight in some strange places.

The yacht left Salonika for Athos without *Solebay* who had two of her sailors missing. She always looked well but the suspicion had grown, after eight warrant punishments in short time, that her company were being driven too hard.

HRH and the male members of his party landed at Athos in the blue and gold of a perfect Aegean day. Mount Athos towered above the yacht while we waited for them. The monastery has been there for over a thousand years, undisturbed by the Turks. No females, human or animal, are allowed there. The library is a treasure house. The royal party were shown a book of flower pictures dating from the ninth century. Our ambassador in Athens had taken it upon himself not to ask the monks for permission for the yacht to land anyone beyond the royal party, although cruise ships had begun to call here.

At Thasos we sat on a terrace and drank coffee and oozou with the olive trees by our heads and the golden light on the fields at our feet. Coloured carpets hung over the white balconies to dry; a troupe of young girls danced to the music of two fiddlers and gave us flowers.

Diary 16th May, 1961 – Thasos to Istanbul

Shivering in whites. Passed into the Dardanelles at 0800. Obelisk memorial and gateway of stone. Turkish destroyer (ex HMS Matchless) *joined the escort and we anchored off Cannakkale at 0900. A great sign on a hill overlooking the*

Narrows says simply '18:3:15', presumably the day when the
battleships failed to force their way through. On the other side
an enormous Turkish soldier with rifle and bayonet is carved
out of the hill side. The British naval attaché said Matchless
had saved his life in Russia.
'What ship?'
'Trinidad.'
'Didn't she torpedo herself?'
'Yes.'
'How can anyone be sure in that sort of dust-up?'
'I was the torpedo officer.'

I walked to Cape Helles over the hillside, left as it was in 1915. A
simple obelisk looks out over the Dardanelles. There are 20,000
names. Below the headland is a small bay honoured by my father's
generation. Lancashire Landing was where the collier *River Clyde*
simply ran her bows ashore and discharged the infantry over
lighters to disaster.

> Then out spake brave Horatius,
>   The Captain of the Gate:
> 'To every man upon this earth
>   Death cometh soon or late.
> And how can man die better
>   Than facing fearful odds,
> For the ashes of his fathers,
>   And the temples of his Gods?'

There is a small garden memorial near the beach with over two
hundred names, mostly Hampshires and Irishmen from the
Munsters. David and Doc Blacklock looked for a record of their
maternal uncles and Doc was successful.

I took a bus over the dirt roads through squalid Turkish villages,
where the little girls wore trousers and bee-eaters and storks

perched on the hovels. We swept into Troy in a dust cloud. I climbed one of the earth mounds and looked over the olive trees to Helles and the peaks of the Greek islands behind. The Troy plain was covered with trees and ditches; small Turkish boys dodged about selling ancient coins and bric-a-brac they had filched from the diggings.

There was a reception at the Turkish Naval HQ on the Golden Horn. Large sailors with bare chests lined the marble staircase and saluted by smacking their hands on to the hilts of their cutlasses. The rooms had glorious chandeliers and painted ceilings. The Turkish admiral's office had an eight feet high ceramic stove and a long table laid out for some conference that had been held there a hundred years before.

The janissaries slow marched, swinging large cutlasses from side to side to clear the way for the sultan, while the drums of their throbbing band terrified the mob. We were given a demonstration and found it hypnotic. The Turks had run an empire much longer than we had and beat us in the straits. One of the military attachés explained.

'Up to battalion level they are superb. They do not move. Their outlook is still that of the rifle and bayonet man despite all the technology. They are man-to-man warriors, off-shoots of the Crimson Horde with an innate barbarism. One of their most infuriating habits is a refusal to accept good advice. They cannot bear not to know already.'

Britannia steamed south back into the Aegean. At Rhodes we found the Greek royal family in their yacht, an ex-Algerian minesweeper re-named *Polymestis*. The Queen, a daughter of the Kaiser, sat on the club fender. Eric, one of the engineer lieutenants, played the guitar and the two princesses and the crown prince talked rapidly in perfect English about sailing. He was an Olympic yachtsman.

We anchored near the entrance where the Colossus of Rhodes bestrode the channel until it fell down in 224 BC. The boatswain exercised the diving party off the breakwater. He told me that they had found a large earthenware jar with two handles on the bottom. It had broken when they tried to get it up. I asked him to draw a picture; it looked like an amphora of antiquity.

Polymestis followed us to Crete and secured in the next berth at Heraklion; a tourist ship was astern. Everyone went ashore to look at Knossos and I stayed on board as duty commander. I had to visit *Polymestis*; her upper deck badly needed a scrub.

The Gloucesters flew home from Suda Bay and our royal duty was at an end. On Jutland Day, 31st May, the wardroom drank Bill Pardy's health. Forty-five years after the battle it is certain that he was the only naval officer survivor from either side still serving at sea. This interesting and harmless episode was not passed on to the media. The rule was no publicity unless unavoidable. An opportunity was missed to generate some good will at a time when the yacht was in need of it. After calls at Malta and Gibraltar we were back in Portsmouth on 5th June.

Chapter 9

BRITISH ISLES AND WEST AFRICA – 1961

BRITANNIA WAS SCHEDULED FOR WEST AFRICA in November and December 1961, to be available to the Queen during her state visit to Ghana. The political situation was delicate; it was decided that the final decision whether she should go would be left to the last moment. Meanwhile the yacht spent the rest of the summer in British waters.

July found us in our old berth in the Pool of London; the members of the wardroom and their wives were invited to a Garden Party at Buckingham Palace. We left that evening with the Queen for her visit to Suffolk. Lord Carrington, the First Lord of the Admiralty was the minister in attendance. At Greenwich the Admiral President and his officers fell in by the waters edge in mess undress to salute the Queen as she went by.

We were met off the Cork Light at Harwich by the Trinity House Vessel *Patricia*. She led us in with our destroyer escort astern while the First Lord sat in the admiral's chair and watched how it was done. We made a dashing run up to the buoy while the admiral gave orders like Gregory Peck and forgot that this First Lord had recently agreed that he be retired, although he had been told that he would get another job.

The Queen landed for her day visit to Suffolk and *Ganges*, the Boys' Training Establishment at Shotley. A garden party was held there that afternoon, attended by the Queen. We had had two happy years at Shotley after the war and my wife came up for it. She told Sue Lee-Barber, an old friend with whom she had spent the night, that she thought the captain of *Ganges* had lovely blue eyes. Sue promptly told him in front of everybody, bringing some fun into the etiquette. Next day we were back at Portsmouth, the Queen left and an enjoyable mini-cruise was over.

My last attendance at Cowes Week began with a press conference in the cruiser *Tiger*, the guardship that year.

Diary 31st July, 1961 – Cowes

Press conference in Tiger. *About thirty there, from all the papers, together with representatives from the foreign warships at Cowes.* Tiger *and the warships virtually ignored. I had to answer a series of unexpected questions about Princess Alexandra. i.e. was she interested in sailing? Had she sailed before? I had no idea but managed to tell them something to keep them happy. No good saying you do not know. Next question would be why are you here? Would dearly have liked to answer with another question, why do you ask? One very interested that Prince Philip was going to the Poona Yacht Club drinks party. No doubt some innuendo will be made out of that. Jack Frost, doyen of the press at Cowes, helpful as ever, but maybe feeling tender. His piece in the* Daily Telegraph *described* Tiger *as a guided missile cruiser. Ours is the only proper navy without one.*

Two motor fishing vessels were laid on to enable the press to watch the sailing. I briefed the officer from *Tiger* in charge of them. They waited until midday when Princess Alexandra went for a sail in a big ketch. The pressmen hung about the ketch too long and I had to flash a 10 inch signal projector on the MFVs to disperse them.

At the end of Cowes week the yacht went to Southampton where the Queen embarked for her Scottish cruise with the Prince and Princess of Hanover and their children. Prince Philip arrived from Cowes half an hour later in a speed boat and we left to go to an anchorage off Yarmouth, Isle of Wight. The Fastnet race was starting and the ocean racers were juggling for position at the line, reefed down because of the weather. When they had gone we left for Milford Haven, arriving the next evening.

I was bidden to dinner and sat on the Queen's left with Prince George on her right. Until half time I exchanged a desultory conversation with an assistant secretary on my left.

'I suppose you went to Dartmouth?'
'No.'
'Where did you go?'
'*Vindictive*, cadet training cruiser.'
'Before that?'
'Are you thinking of offering me a job? I can give you my CV.'
'What do you think my job is worth?'
'Five hundred a year on an open market.'

Prince George commanded a squadron of cavalry in Russia for three years. Apparently horses could cover ground unsuitable for armoured vehicles. He told me that he had served under Guderian, the prince of open warfare. It was fascinating to hear him.

The yacht visited Ramsey Island, by St David's Head. A five to six knot tide rip went through the channel. To the south lay a hideous line of rocks known as the Bitches; a submerged rock called Horse Rock lay in mid channel. Buzzards hovered over the island carrying rabbits into the air and dropping them when they felt hungry. The island was rented by a farmer who let rooms to holidaymakers; they were surprised to find themselves engaged in conversation by the Queen.

During a two day visit to Belfast and Bangor the Queen carried out her engagements ashore, Prince Philip entered a yacht race and the wardroom played golf. The sternsheetsman in the royal barge fell over the side, while the rain came relentlessly down.

Britannia spent a day at anchor in Horse Sound, Ross and Cromarty, for a private three day visit by the Queen to the Marquess and Marchioness of Linlithgow, and then on to Loch Laxford, a long narrow loch surrounded by low islands with two 2000 feet hills at its head. Here the concert party performed, with the help of Charles and Anne who came on as a doctor and nurse to examine Leading Cook Collier for a spaceman.

'Well, what do you think nurse?'

'I think he is very good-looking.'

He was, and it made the audience laugh.

The sailmaker was very funny, as usual and as usual we all cringed in case he crossed the line. The Queen laughed throughout his turn so we felt safe in assuming that he had got away with it once more. Jock Slater, a future First Sea Lord, took his career in his hands when he borrowed the admiral's reefer and pince-nez spectacles and gave a near perfect impression of the scene on the bridge on a day when things did not go quite right.

In the wardroom after the show, the factor to the 100,000 acre Westminster estate cornered me and reported that two sailors from *Paladin*, the yacht's escort destroyer, had borrowed one of Her Grace's dinghies to get back to their ship. We recovered the boat, gave him a drink and sent him on his way, more sad than angry, murmuring about the disturbance being caused to the salmon and red deer. The captain of *Paladin* was delighted that his sailors should be so anxious not to break their leave that they were prepared to borrow a boat to get back. The yacht was in no position to point the finger at *Paladin*.

Diary 13th August, 1961 – Loch Laxford

During last night's royal concert it has transpired that many of the chiefs went fishing; others asked for a film.

We anchored in Thurso Bay to enable the royal party to visit the Queen Mother at the Castle of Mey. The castle made a romantic sight, floodlit with the royal standard flying. The Queen and the royal party left at Macduff. Five weeks later *Britannia* was on her way to West Africa.

The plan for the Queen's visit to Ghana could not be confirmed until the government at home was satisfied that the political situation there was sufficiently stable; meanwhile the yacht steamed south to be ready if required.

At Las Palmas our lines were taken by a party from the destroyer *Diana*, commanded by an officer with three DSCs. The admiral was displeased by the rubber tyred fenders there, which should have been replaced by the berthing party before they marked our glossy blue sides.

We found Freetown in a buzz of anticipation in the hoped-for visit of the Queen on the way back from her Ghana tour. Vultures on the cranes watched us come alongside. The flagpoles were going up and the houses were freshly painted.

The day before our scheduled arrival in Ghana President Nkruma's statue had its feet blown off by dissident elements in Accra. Duncan Sandys, the Commonwealth Secretary, squeezed into the back of a Canberra day bomber to make a last minute check there and we continued to Takoradi to await the decision from Westminster. The admiral proposed that if the tour was called off the yacht should go on to Lagos rather than return to Freetown. We were told that return to Freetown was the only acceptable alternative. No reason was given and we hoped for the best. Two bombs went off in Accra that day but the government accepted the Commonwealth Secretary's advice that the royal visit should go ahead.

Takoradi provided a bonus. The facilities for the yachtsmen had been arranged by the naval officer-in-charge, a former yacht officer who had come round the world with us in 1959. Rodney knew what was required during our short stay and had laid on an excellent welcome. It was part of his job to start up a navy for Ghana but the difficulties were great. The RN officers he had been given were predictably not in the first eleven and when he promoted Ghanaians they had no sense of responsibility except to themselves. Over all lay the pall of national corruption and graft.

Ghana was an important pawn in the cold war. The Russians were trying to set up a large naval base at the new port of Sekondi, near Takoradi. Rodney's mission to train a Ghanaian navy was a counter to the Russian strategy. The visit of the Queen in *Britannia* helped to influence the course the newly independent Ghana followed.

Diary 8th November, 1961 – Tema

Arrived Tema, a brand new port built by Parkinson Howard and built very well. Berths almost empty and the wired compounds filled with new machinery beginning to rust amidst the advancing jungle grass. Attended the admiral at lunch with our high commissioner. The driver said he knew the way but he did not and we were twenty minutes late. Admiral not impressed by the brand new house, G-plan furniture and our pro-consul, who did not inspire him with confidence.
'Did you see his shoes? In Egypt Lord Lloyd had four ADCs and a Rolls-Royce with four Union Jacks. Lady Lloyd told me that one of the ADCs would have to be sent home because he talked about "lunch".'
Dance in the evening at the Ministry of Defence mess. Shiny black faces in red mess kit, enormous negresses and dead beat white officers doing little. Commodore Hansen, young Ghanaian is head of the navy. Affable chap with a mutilated eye he got from his own side in the Congo.

The Queen arrived by air and the visit was officially on. She was not expected to embark in the yacht for eleven days.

Three thousand men of the Ghana army and police paraded before the 100,000 spectators at Black Horse Square. A front line of four hundred scarlet coated soldiers stood in the sun before the Gate of Freedom and Justice. A throng of women in gold cloth robes carried babies, walking behind the chiefs with umbrella carriers and mace bearers. The spectators cheered wildly whenever the line of soldiers was called to attention. They were more interested than vociferous when the Queen went by. Now and again the black faces gave way to the sunburned skin and ramrod figure of a British NCO, sheepdogs at the corners of the flock that they had trained like guardsmen. The drill and dressing was good by any standard despite the thick scarlet tunics and grilling sun.

Jock and I found ourselves guests at Accra races. There were six races and in all but two of them a jockey was fined or suspended for pulling his horse, barging or some other offence laid down by the Jockey Club, far, far away. The horses were small and the jockeys looked enormous. At the start of one race a jockey put his head over the wires of the starting gate. When it went up he was lifted out of the saddle and landed on the ground behind his horse, then vanishing round the track without him.

The wait at Tema kept the wardroom at full throttle with social engagements, almost entirely with the local Europeans; the culture divide between us and the Ghanaians was hard to bridge, although both sides did their best. We felt sometimes that there was a challenge in the air. At one dinner party given by senior army officers and their wives and mistresses the general announced that he had been commisioned from the ranks and in his opinion any officer, of any service, who had not been through the ranks was not much good. His colleagues agreed at once, even the Sandhurst trained ones, anxious to keep on side with the boss. They had backed Nkruma into power and wanted to be by the right chair when the music stopped next time.

David and I set off for Takoradi to spend a night out of the ship with Rodney. On the way we swam off a beach reserved in times past for the British officers of the Holt Line ships trading to the Gold Coast. It was a 140 mile drive and the dirt road risky, with occasional unlit Mammy trucks parked on it.

Rodney was busy getting ready for the Queen, who would embark in the yacht there. His gunner's mate found it difficult to drill the royal guard of seaman on the asphalt parade ground. The sun melted the tar and rendered the guard immobile, however loudly they were shouted at.

We borrowed his staff car and driver and set out for the return to Tema. The road at Cape Coast was blocked for the Queen's arrival and we were held up. The telephone at the nearest African hotel was not working. I got through to the ship after a long walk to the post office, dug into a corner of Cape Coast castle. The post office counter was piled high with old heaps of paper, faded by the sun, while queues of patient customers talked cheerfully among themselves and wondered at two white men trying to telephone in the middle of the day.

Outside the post office we were met by the Queen's motorcade. We bowed amidst the throng as she went past although we knew she would not recognise us; no question would arise why two senior officers from *Britannia* were a hundred miles from their place of duty, apparently lost in an old centre of slavery on the Gold Coast.

Rodney was anxious to have his car back as soon as possible. When we finished with it at Tema I told the leading seaman driver to go back to Takoradi and report to the commander as soon as he could get there. His English was reasonable and he understood. Rodney did not see him for two weeks. He went to his village up country to show his family the new foul anchor on his sleeve and take them for rides in the staff car.

Diary 5th November, 1961 – Tema

At 0745 the merchantman Ashanti Palm *clouted us aft while manoeuvering in the basin in a squall. She had two tugs but they failed to hold her. At lunch time the master, a serious Scot, came over. He was used to going 600 miles up the Niger River. He described how his bridge got lost in the trees. He was contrite that he should have picked our ship, among all others, to have hit. The press were soon on. The master denied that he had hit us! (Sounds like his owners' insurers denying liability.) I put out what happened – Yacht alongside – merchant ship touched us while manoeuvering with tugs in a squall – accident – trivial incident.*
Daily Telegraph *have a front page story making out the tugs to be heroes instead of fools and we were to blame in some way.* Times *similar. Conference for Ghanaian press on the jetty. They seemed to understand but might pretend they haven't and file anything to titillate the readership.*

The president laid on a ball for two thousand to celebrate the Queen's last night in Ghana. It was held under coloured lights in the garden of the State House. The president attempted a dance with the Queen but had to give it up because of the crush which formed around them. Accompanied by clapping they left the floor led by the robust figure of Superintendant Kelly, the Queen's detective.

The Pakistan High Commissioner was there with his beautiful wife, the daughter of a maharajah, and I continued a conversation about Kashmir which we had begun before. I heard about the gardens at Shalimar, the lakes and the people who are so poor that they wear a pot of warm coal round their necks in the winter so that they will not freeze. They are known by the black marks they have on their chests. I asked her to pronounce 'Srinagar' and I can hear it now.

Shortly before we left the next morning a consignment of generous gifts arrived from the Osagyefo, or president. I was given an Ashanti kante cloth in red and gold, sandals and a set of Ghana stamps. All the senior officers were treated similiarly.

The yacht anchored briefly off Black Star Steps, Accra, for the fireworks. We were asked to darken ship so that the fireworks could be seen at their best against the night sky. *Britannia* oiled at sea during the night and secured alongside at Takoradi in the early morning to await the Queen.

The jetty was rigged with tiered stands, flags, palm pots and numerous sweepers brushing the dust skywards. The Queen arrived with the president for the farewell lunch. Fifty-four sat down. The admiral complained to me afterwards that the locals with pro-Russian leanings behaved badly, lounging about their chairs and even shouting remarks at the British High Commissioner.

During the afternoon the stands filled up with all colours of kante clothes, the chiefs with silk umbrellas, mace bearers, drummers, children, hornblowers and occasional wives. Rodney's royal guard from the Ghana navy marched on attended by the chief petty officer RN who had trained them, and commanded by an RN officer. Ninety-nine black faces and one white went through their drill with precision and verve. The president made a speech and the Queen brought floods of applause in her reply by referring to Ghana as the senior African member of the Commonwealth. She walked ashore, shook hands with the president and when she came back we were off in short time, escorted by two Ghanaian navy inshore minesweepers. The end of the jetty was lined with schoolgirls in green dresses waving goodbye with Ghanaian flags. They were the hope for the future. Outside our old friend *Saintes* and the frigate *Jaguar* joined us for the voyage to Monrovia.

The admiral exercised the two escorts with *Britannia* in some of the evolutions that were part of daily life in the days when he commanded a destroyer squadron. He knew of course that he

141

would be leaving the yacht and the navy at the end of the cruise and he would never again command ships at sea.

Diary 23rd November, 1961 – Takoradi to Monrovia

Royal Squadron came up to Monrovia, the capital of the negro republic of Liberia. The president's yacht, commanded by a dashing Spaniard, approached our starboard bow at a brisk speed and carrying plenty of wheel. She was dressed forward only and firing a royal salute. She charged up to the yacht, tucked herself under our stern, forcing Jaguar *to haul quickly out of the line.*

Signals:

Britannia *to steam yacht: 'Keep clear.'*
Steam yacht to Britannia*: 'Please go slower.'*
She finished up behind Solebay *and could not keep up. For the sake of harmony we slowed down, causing the line to straggle.*

The jetty was full of soldiers, bandsmen and negroes in blue uniforms covered in gold braid. President Tubman arrived to welcome the Queen in top hat and morning coat, smeared in medals.

The garden party was held at the British Embassy on asphalt dusted with sand. I met a steel erector from Middlesborough putting in the steelwork for President Tubman's latest house, a South African electrical engineer and Marconi's man in Liberia. The Queen and Prince Philip arrived and steered stoically through the crush.

The country was set up by the generosity of the Americans, determined to bring a negro democracy to Africa. The women in the political class get their clothes in Paris and educate their children in England. One of them made it clear that they despise things American and regard themselves as Europeans living in West Africa.

The president invited the Queen to a farewell reception at the palace and members of the wardroom were there. For the first time we enjoyed the Edwardian image of yacht service – sipping champagne and watching the fireworks at court.

Diary 25 November, 1961 – Freetown

Entered Freetown harbour in column. Shore crowded. Off King Tom a flotilla of decorated bullom boats with shouting Africans blowing horns to greet the Queen. On the jetty a smart guard of the 1st Sierra Leone Regiment in khaki shorts, red fez and waistcoats. African sergeant-major went down the line with a pace stick. The British brigadier had the DSO and MC and the lieutenant-colonel two MCs. The Queen landed, coolly dressed in ice blue and inspected the guard before receiving a long line of dignitaries standing on the jetty in strict order of precedence. Vice-Admiral Sir Nicholas Copeman, the C-in-C South Atlantic, stood about twentieth in the line, immaculate in white uniform under the cranes, while the vultures on the shed stretched their hairless necks to watch the show. This is how the wind of change blows in Africa. When Evans of the Broke was C-in-C in the twenties he started a war in West Africa on his own.

Parade later first class. Soldiers looked fit and business-like, askaris with mostly British officers. Band smart and lively and the colour ceremony moving and well done. The Queen marvellous, looking with an expert eye on her regiment from the Land Rover. A diversion when a party of locals fell out of a tree into a crowded stand.

Solebay precariously alongside King Tom pier with an anchor down. At low water she has a list and must be aground. She is useful there for running the canteen and providing a shore telephone link. I jumped for her gangway and the swell whipped the boat against the ladder, taking a piece out of her gunwale. Missed my left foot by a whisker. David said he thought I had had it. Told him a little more concern would have been in order.

The Queen returned after her tour up-country and that evening there was the usual farewell ceremony on the jetty. By the time it was over the light had begun to go. The admiral switched on the floodlighting on board and the crowd cheered and clapped. The squadron took a wide sweep in the harbour and *Jaguar*, the last ship in the column, came in for some attention.

Fory to *Jaguar*: 'Get into station.'

Fory to *Jaguar*: 'What is the matter?'

She had engine trouble and trailed astern for several hours.

On passage to the Gambia the escort steamed past and cheered ship. *Solebay* and *Saintes* looked particularly well and the admiral tried to persuade captain (D) in *Solebay* to bring the squadron closer to *Britannia* but he was not persuaded. *Saintes* fired a pattern of live squid. *Britannia* turned round and stopped in the pattern looking for fish. We saw none. *Saintes* went after a turtle which got away.

The holiday mood went on. That evening four wardroom officers dined aft. We waited in the anteroom as usual but the Queen did not arrive. An equerry came in and said the the Queen wished to see the admiral alone in her sitting room. I jumped to the conclusion that he was for it and my mind leapt over the possibilities. Could it be the *Jaguar* breakdown which marred yesterday's departure? Or the racket from the squid firing? Or the fun and games looking for fish in the pattern? Quite wrong. To his surprise the admiral was knighted and made a Knight Commander of the Royal Victorian Order.

After dinner the Queen decided not to attend the film. She described to the admiral and me a play she had seen twice with

Cecily Courtneidge in it. She thought it hilarious and gave an imitation of her part in the show, swinging her arms and imitating Cecily Courtneidge's walk. It was extremely funny. It was a memorable evening.

Bathurst was the capital of a colony of 200,000 Africans and 200 whites. It has a place in history as a collection centre for slaves on the way to the Americas. They were gathered in Fort James, built on an island in the Gambia River and conveniently placed for their journey. Despite these sombre associations the locals seemed cheerful. A cool wind from the Sahara blows over them and reduces the sea temperature, which may help.

The following day *Britannia* shifted berth to Muta Point, forty miles up the Gambia River and the Queen and Prince Philip set off in the motor cutter to explore, intending to rejoin the main river further up, where the yacht would go to meet them. The tributaries were of varying depths; the motor cutter was chosen in preference to the barge because it drew less water.

The expedition was led by the motor cutter, followed by a jolly boat and two motor boats as escorts. We went through a succession of mangrove swamps, their long roots covered in oyster shells. The trees were filled with parrots and the water's edge with pelicans, cranes, ibis and herons. They made no attempt to get away. A wedge of crested cranes flew fifty feet over us, with red and blue bullseyes and tufts behind their heads. Mud fish flopped about. Prince Philip shot a ten foot crocodile ahead as the channel narrowed. A fallen mangrove tree almost blocked the stream. We saw the motor cutter's crew trying to clear it while the other boats stopped. The tree was immovable. The motor cutter managed to skate past one end and then it was our turn. There could be no question of the motor boats getting through because of their draft; David shouted that he was going back to the ship with the motor boats and I was now in charge of the escort and responsible for getting the royal party back to the yacht. I was conscious of the growing dark, the blocked channel and the presence of the Queen in the boat on the other side of the block.

A strong tide was beginning to run and the first two shots at the barrier were unsuccessful. I told the coxswain to go further downstream and get a good run at the end of the tree, using more power. We touched the bank and got through in a shower of black mud. I followed the motor cutter into a wider tributary and we were back an hour later.

The fourteen officers who were leaving before the Queen next came to *Britannia* were summoned to say goodbye. We went in individually to the Queen's sitting room where she and Prince Philip were standing.

'That is a smart set of Number Tens.'

'The laundry's best, sir'

'You've been here some time, haven't you?'

'I came in '58, ma'am.'

'Where will you go next?'

'Instructor at the Staff College, Greenwich, ma'am.'

'We should like you to have this photograph as a souvenir of your service here.'

'Thank you very much, ma'am.'

Afterwards the leavers had a farewell drink with the household. Adeane told a funny story about the Foreign Secretary's tiger shoot. Apparently Lord Home kept missing and the tiger got browned off and drifted into the bush.

Diary 5th December, 1961 – Bathurst to Dakar

Firework display after dinner. Sailed for Dakar at 2030. The admiral took her in a sweep very close to the jetty where HRH and the governor were standing (HRH leaving here for Tanganyika independence celebrations). Bugles sounded the Hausa farewell and we went past fast and close, the stern swinging in. It was risky and impressive.

At Dakar the Queen was greeted by a guard of Senegalese paras and a visit by the president. The president accompanied her to inspect the guard and shortly afterwards she left us to fly home looking very lovely in a particularly attractive hat.

When she had gone the admiral cleared lower deck and read out to the yachtsmen a message of thanks from the Queen and told them that she had ordered that the main brace be spliced in all the ships of the squadron. He knew that his years of royal service were over and he would no longer be able to offer the remarkable loyalty and devotion to the sovereign which had been a keystone in his life.

Diary 6th December, 1961 – Dakar

We hung about until 1230 when we saw the Boeing 707 take off with the Queen. Admiral reluctant to go, making excuses about other ships being in the way, unable to accept that the Queen no longer needed him. The big jet did not have to turn back and landed six hours later in December London. We left for Portsmouth and got there after sixteen days.

The admiral took the ship up harbour to H moorings at Whale Island. He left the bridge for the last time and the wardroom drank his health in champagne. Some had mixed feelings but I did not share them. I knew what his contribution had been.

Chapter 10

CRUISE OF HRH THE PRINCESS ROYAL TO THE MEDITERRANEAN 1962

THIS WAS MY LAST CRUISE IN BRITANNIA. I was the only member of the 1958 wardroom still there. Only two of us were left among those who accompanied HRH The Princess Royal to the West Indies in 1960. The turnover in officers was brisk. The seagoing ships in the navy were reducing but Britannia steamed on, an unlikely target for the politicians' axe until old age condemned her. She provided a sea job in times when they were becoming rare; this added to her attraction to naval officers facing careers with rising periods of desk time ashore.

Sheila drove me to South Railway Jetty for the last time on the 12th February 1962.

'Shall I wait?'

'Why?'

'You can't go in this.'

'That is what I'm paid for.'

'The Royals aren't.'

She had a point. It was difficult to talk in the gale. The yacht was being pushed on to the jetty with her flags and dressing lines gusting stiffly out at right angles. The brow to the shore creaked as she moved in the howling wind. The new admiral, Rear Admiral J. C. C. Henley, was taking her to sea for the first time. He decided to wait twenty-four hours in the hope that the blow in the channel would ease. Meanwhile the Princess and the same mature entourage that came with her last time walked round the *Victory*.

The sea and swell hit her as soon as we left the shelter of the Isle of Wight. The weather was on the bow and in those conditions *Britannia* pitched abominably. The stabilisers made it worse, acting as a kind of fulcrum to the pitching. The wardroom was almost empty for lunch and dinner and the admiral was not seen on the bridge until the second day. The new boys with small ship experience told the old hands what they already knew – this ship was unpleasant in a seaway on the bow.

During our days working for the controller, Admiral Dawnay and I were invited to try a ship motion simulator at a guided weapons range. It was called a rolling platform and the name was appropriate. We agreed that it beat any destroyer in a gale. *Britannia* was, at her most venomous, in that class.

Two of us answered an invitation from the household and were met by Admiral Sir Geoffrey and Lady Margaret Hawkins and Major Eastwood; the others were still recuperating but these three were in sparkling form. Lady Margaret had heard her husband's yarns before.

'I was given an urgent sea job and never did subs courses.'

'You seem to have dodged all kinds of things.'

The bad weather returned as we neared Gibraltar.

Diary 16th February, 1962 – Portsmouth to Gibraltar

Bad night. Ploughing now into easterly gale. She pitched madly until 0400 when we had to reduce speed. Arrival time went from 1000 to 1330 then 1530. We hardly made good seven knots. Sea white with spray and very short waves. Anchored off Gib breakwater at 1530. Sea covered with squall effects – spray whipped about and curling all over the place. Shifted inside to a buoy when it had gone down a little. Unable to get alongside until 0800 next morning.

HRH went to church in Gibraltar Cathedral and the wardroom turned up in support. The first lesson was read by the Flag Officer Gibraltar and the second by the governor. The dean made a gracious reference to royalty before his sermon which reverberated in the high roof and boomed down all round us but lost the message, which had something to do with astronomy. My tweed suit was not on. Gibraltar does not rate itself as the country and the locals were in dark suits. They were doing well with new cars, full shops and plenty to eat.

The wardroom hired a bus and visited a sherry bodega at Jerez de la Frontiera owned by a be-spectacled OE called the Marques del Merito. After a long tasting session near the alligators in the garden we came back by the coast road through Algeciras and La Linea. The stale poverty everywhere was depressing. In each town square we were pestered by small boys touting their sisters to anyone with modest resources and inclination. The bus driver kept up a constant 30 mph and took his foot off the throttle every time he touched the radio. He knew that Gibraltarian bus drivers would not be popular with the Spanish police.

I was summoned to dine with HRH and afterwards to a concert given by the Hungarian Refugee Orchestra in the Naval Cinema. Afterwards she presented the Governor and Lady Keightley with a silver salver, to their surprise and evident delight. She was a popular figure everywhere.

Five days in Gibraltar was plenty and most were glad to leave for Famagusta. Gibraltar ran an empire routine of make believe. It provided a constant look-back to what we once were. Over the border the Spanish in their poverty looked on with contempt.

The yacht did not go into Valletta but cruised along the north coast of Malta. The governor was unwilling to let us enter harbour because a general election was imminent. The battery at St Elmo fired a royal salute and the 108th Minesweeping Flotilla passed down our starboard side with their hands manning ship; four small wooden boats represented the Mediterranean Fleet.

We ran close in along the north coast and I saw Pace's House again, a villa on top of the hill at Maddelena which we shared with the Shaws in the early fifties. When *Gravelines* went by Bill Shaw would close the land and burn a signal projector, while Sheila and Mollie stood on the balcony with the children and waved a sheet at us. It was only eleven years before but the Mediterranean Fleet then had an aircraft carrier squadron, a cruiser squadron, destroyers, frigates, submarines and minesweepers.

> Nothing beside remains. Round the decay
> Of that colossal wreck, boundless and bare,
> The lone and level sands stretch far away.

Diary 1 March, 1962 – Famagusta

Harbour very small with a castle bearing down on one side. We arrived three hours early to get the advantage of the calm at dawn. A guard of honour of indigenous soldiers shambled on to the jetty with their tin hats on the wrong way round. The yacht manned ship, our band played the anthems and HRH dutifully inspected the guard.

This was what the loss of empire comes to – a king's daughter being asked to inspect a rabble. Invited to a party with the army at Dekelia. Met Noel Shead, a Chindit, who led the bayonet charge on Hill 2171 when Blaker got his V.C. All this is described in Master's The Road Past Mandalay. *He thought Masters a good soldier but the Chindit campaign was never on.*

The President, Archbishop Makarios, and the Vice-President, Doctor Kutchuk, lunched with HRH. Our escort frigate, *Scarborough*, fired the appropriate gun salutes of twenty-one and

151

nineteen guns. The vice-president arrived late and someone else got his gun salute. We never found out who it was. No one seemed to mind.

That evening HRH gave a reception. I was in full song about the glories of ancient Greece to a glum audience of visitors. One of the men said that they were all Turks. I shifted quickly to the charms of Istanbul and they cheered up. My patter about the janissaries and Turkish coffee went down alright. A beautiful Turkish girl said that the coffee should be brought to the boil once, not three times as I had been told. An elderly English expatriate harpooned me with reminiscences about the jollity in Limassol forty years before, when Admiral Dawnay and Prince George of Greece were midshipmen in the Mediterranean Fleet and she was a slip of a gal.

Diary 3rd March, 1962 – Famagusta

Duty commander. A sapper major with a large moustache came on board at lunchtime. He was once port commandant at Christmas Island and came for a chat. Only two of us able to talk about that visit. High Commissioner to dinner with HRH. They brought their daughter too and I took her to the wardroom to talk to the four duty officers. Her car arrived and I went to the gangway to see her over the side. Eastwood, in front of her, asked me if I would escort her to a dance at Dekeilia. Admiral butted in and said he thought his duty commander should stay on board. One of the watch-keepers got the job. I saw them off, not sure whether I had won or lost. Before going below I had to repel a drunken merchant seaman from the ship astern. He thought we were a nightclub.

Three of us went to Kyrenia with the admiral via Nicosia and travelled the infamous Ledra Street where terrorists shot soldiers and policemen in the back. Now the men drinking under the trees smiled as we went by. At Bellapaix Abbey, built by the French on their route to the Crusades, weeds grew in the walls and the golden light which seems to hang over everything in this part of the world shone through the rose windows and over the honey coloured stone. We lunched on the roof of the Harbour Club, used by the Household Cavalry during the troubles as their mess, and went round the castle. The vaulted galleries look over the sea with white light cutting through the archery slits built to the glory of God by the Crusaders on the way to Palestine. Some religion, some army.

On the way back we called for a drink at the flower farm of a retired soldier. He told me that he had made a pile during the troubles, selling flowers for the funerals.

After two days' delay because of the weather we moved to Limassol. A party given by the RAF was solid with senior army officers. The red tabs were everywhere in full song about their trips to Greece, sailing, skiing and arranging to keep their lives interesting; the rump of empire.

At HRH's evening reception a Greek woman asked to be presented. She had given a bouquet to the Princess in 1937, when she was a little girl. I passed her on to Admiral Hawkins who bent down and cupped his ear. Unfortunately he got it wrong and thanked her profusely for bringing flowers. It ended happily and she was presented.

On passage to Tobruk the bad weather followed us. We had two anchors down in Limassol and met a heavy north west swell outside. During the night HRH was injured when a door closed on her foot, badly bruising it and breaking a vein. The squadron altered to a course across the swell to enable her to get down to the sick bay for an X-ray. She made it clear that there would be no alterations to her programme although she must have been very uncomfortable after a trying passage.

I invited the coxswain, chief yeoman of signals and chief writer to my cabin to say thank you and goodbye over a farewell drink. Chief Yeoman Fisher, DSM and bar, explained his angle:

'I am sorry you are going. I know exactly how far I can go with you and now I have to begin again with your relief.'

I was last in Tobruk in February 1952 and remember looking out of the wardroom scuttle of *Armada* and asking whose funeral was on because the cruiser *Glasgow* had her jack at half-mast. We learned then that King George VI had died. A monolithic fort now stood on the eastern side in honour of the dead of the Africa Corps; on the other side there was a new palace for the Libyan royal family.

The Crown Prince called on HRH and as he stepped over the side his standard was broken and the flags brought down simultaneously from the other two masts. At the same time the gunsmoke of the first gun of the royal salute shot out from *Scarborough*. It would have made a good picture if someone like Van der Velde could have painted it.

HRH, Lady Margaret Hawkins and Miss Gwynneth Lloyd, her lady-in-waiting, were dined by the wardroom. After dinner the Princess sat with her injured foot on a stool and charmed us as she always did with anecdotes from her life. The weather had been bad enough to affect the sailors but she was never heard to mention it, let alone complain. It had been my good fortune to serve in the ship for two cruises with her and watch how she did the things that mattered. She was a Victorian with no problems about her duty to her House and her country.

Diary 14th March, 1962 – Tobruk

Visited the war graves. British; beautifully kept headstones in rows, trees, alcoves, a cross or two and a brave attempt at gardens. The ashes of 7,000 German soldiers are buried in a sandstone castle keep. Their names, without rank or unit, line the alcoves. A down draft wind whistled over the high walls round the courtyard. A cold unsentimental place, full of ghosts. One page of the visitors book covered with anti-German abuse; another, in German, to the effect that the sacrifice did not matter; Hitler was to be blamed because he failed. The Italians had a cemetery but it was desecrated by Arabs. Fifty years on, who won and who lost will begin to fade. The brotherhood of the front line stays.

A reception ashore to be given by the RAF had to be cancelled. An easterly gale covered the anchorage with clouds of dust and sand. Our boats could not be recovered until 0330 when they were hoisted in a lull and we left while the going was good. Outside *Scarborough* was detached and we ran before the wind for Tripoli.

The wardroom invited me to dinner to say good bye but the weather on both the nights on passage made it impossible. My last day at sea in *Britannia* was spent in a full gale. The wind went down later in the day and we managed to increase speed to 15 knots and get to Tripoli at our estimated time of arrival. My relief appeared and we began the turnover. I was summoned to lunch by the Princess to say goodbye and the wardroom, chief petty officers and petty officers entertained me to farewell drinks; I left at dawn the following morning to catch the aeroplane.

About two hours into the flight the senior air hostess arrived in tears and complained to a short fair-haired young officer next to me that two of his highlanders were now drunk and fighting. He left without a word. Five minutes later he was back in his seat with his book. The shouts changed to sobbing. A Scottish soldier shambled along the aisle and mumbled an apology and was told curtly to sit down and shut up.

It was good to be back.

EPILOGUE

BRITANNIA'S LIFE ON THE ACTIVE LIST ended at about 1530 on the 11th December 1997 when the Commodore Royal Yachts saluted his ship and ordered her colours to be lowered. The band on the jetty played the Sunset Hymn.

> The day Thou gavest, Lord, is ended,
> The darkness falls at Thy behest.

He saluted the Queen and the band played the National Anthem; his job was done. Some there, among the many who had manned *Britannia,* and their families, cried, perhaps because she was going, or because of the setting and the hymn and the beauty of the ship before them.

I thought about her great days in the Seaway and what a bitch she had been when the weather was on the bow. Now her time had arrived after a long and honourable run. When her Union Flag came down the show was really over. Her flag was a symbol, a marker for all those that had been lowered, throughout the empire, while she had been in commission.

Perched on my football stand on that freezing winter afternoon, I felt again pride in the men of my old service who had manned her, willingly exchanging the military life for which they had been trained, for royal duty, where the game had to be played with a soft ball. The elegant figure of the commodore, the immobile lines of yachtsmen, the drill and music of the band before the old painted lady were reminders that for forty-four years the standard had not changed.

Historians will say that she was an anachronism, built when the navy and the empire were in decline, when it was obvious that while the glory was still there the power was fast draining away. She was laid down when the Queen came to the throne at the age of twenty-five, one of the tokens of a new Elizabethan Age. Much has since turned to ashes; the cynics argue that the Royal Navy is now a handful of men and women sea fencibles with an apocalyptic bomb. Amidst all this *Britannia* was always a bright ember to remind my generation of the pride in the past and hope for the future that we had when we were young.